PRAISE FOR
SUSTAINABLE BADASS

"Gittemarie is a one-of-a-kind creator and a much-needed voice in the movement. Her attention to detail and level of research is a true testament not only to the quality of her work, but to the intensity with which she takes on the waste crisis. A much-respected and positive force!"

—Immy Lucas (@Sustainably_Vegan)

"Gittemarie is creator that not only provides helpful tips on living a zero-waste and vegan lifestyle, but also articulates it in way that is approachable."

—Jhánneu Roberts (@Jhanneu)

"Gittemarie provides extensive amounts of accessible eco-friendly tips and education for those entering a sustainability lifestyle. With themed recipes and fun humor, Gittemarie is paving the way for sustainable futures."

—Isaias Hernandez (@QueerBrownVegan)

"*Sustainable Badass* is enlightening and entertaining! It'll have you reaching for your reusable bags and turning that eco-guilt into action."

—Kathryn Kellogg, author of *101 Ways to Go Zero Waste* (@going. zero.waste)

"Gittemarie has been an inspiration to me for years! She's always prepared to address a given environmental concern with an educated perspective and provide solutions to her audience. Not to mention her style, which makes her my personal favorite eco-fashionista."

—Shelbi Orme (@shelbizleee)

SUSTAINABLE
BADASS

SUSTAINABLE BADASS

A Zero-Waste Lifestyle Guide

GITTEMARIE JOHANSEN

CORAL GABLES

Cover Design: Elina Diaz
Interior Illustration: Tsvetina
Production Design (English): Katia Mena
Translation: Gittemarie Johansen, Jens Damborg Jens,
and Christian Bredvig Fjordside

For permission requests, please contact the publisher at:
Mango Publishing Group
2850 S Douglas Road, 4th Floor
Coral Gables, FL 33134 USA
info@mango.bz

For special orders, quantity sales, course adoptions and corporate sales, please email the publisher at sales@mango.bz. For trade and wholesale sales, please contact Ingram Publisher Services at customer.service@ingramcontent.com or +1.800.509.4887.

Sustainable Badass: A Zero-Waste Lifestyle Guide

Library of Congress Cataloging-in-Publication number: 2021952881
ISBN: (print) 978-1-64250-869-7, (ebook) 978-1-64250-870-3
BISAC category code HOM022000, HOUSE & HOME / Sustainable Living

Printed in the United States of America

Table of Contents

Foreword 14

Preface 16

Chapter 1—The Plastic Problem **19**

    This Is How Plastic Is Made 20

    Microplastic 22

    Garbage Islands 24

    What Are We Doing about It? 29

Chapter 2—Recycling: A Waste-Management Guide **30**

    How Is Plastic Recycled? 31

    What about Bioplastic? 34

    How Is Organic Waste Recycled? 36

    How Is Glass Recycled? 37

    How Is Paper Recycled? 40

    How Is Metal Recycled? 42

    What about Return Systems? 43

Chapter 3—Going Green: Working Toward Zero Waste **46**

    How I Got Started 48

    A Beginner's Guide 50

    You Cannot Buy Your Way Out of the Climate Crisis ... 53

    How Do You Avoid Greenwashing? 55

        Tips for avoiding greenwashing 56

Chapter 4—The Plastic You Cannot Avoid **61**

Chapter 5—A Zero-Waste Household **63**

    Homemade Cleaning Supplies 65

        Dish soap 69

Brushes and cloths 69

Alternatives to Foil and Film 71

Toilet paper 73

Recipe for Toilet Tabs 75

Laundry 76

Compost Guide 78

Worm compost 79

Chapter 6—Electronics **83**

E-Waste and Disposal 84

Pre-Loved Gadgets 85

Planned Obsolescence and Repairs 86

Data Storage and Streaming 90

Greener habits online 92

Chapter 7—Clothing **93**

What Is Fast Fashion? 94

How to Spot the Sustainable Brands 100

1. Do they have actual certificates to back up
   their claims? 101

2. Is the supply chain transparent? 102

3. Is there consistency between the price and
   the product? 102

4. Can you get in touch with the brand? 102

Kicking the Habit of Fast Fashion 103

Secondhand and Clothing Swaps 105

Gittemarie's guide to thrift shops 107

Clothing swaps and secondhand apps 108

Repairs and Maintenance 109

Tips for the Minimalist Wardrobe 110

Fashion Mentality and Designer Labels 112

Materials and Textiles 115

What are the most sustainable materials? 120

Chapter 8—**Food and Grocery Shopping** **123**

Animal Agriculture 127

Imported Feed 130

Zero-Waste Meat? 131

What about White Meat and Fish? 133

Facts about bottom trawling 134

What Should We Eat Instead? 136

Commonly heard statements about animal products
and some solutions 136

Sustainable Lunches 143

Wax wrap 143

Lunchbox 143

Glass jars 144

Canvas bags 144

Water bottles and canteens 144

Cutlery 145

Your own box for salads 146

Snacks 146

Bringing Your Own Container—A Guide to Politeness 146

Chapter 9—**Kitchen Guide** **150**

Useful and Plastic-Free Ingredients to Have in the Kitchen 151

Seasonal Greens 153

Food Storage 155

In and out of the fridge 155

The freezer 156

Food Waste 158

How to Buy Groceries without Any Trash 159

Conventional Supermarkets 162

My Favorite Recipes 165

    Birthday Buns 165

    Burger Buns 167

    Vegan Meringue 168

    Carrot Cake 169

    Homemade Oat Milk 170

    Green Ravioli with Nut Filling 171

    Plant-Based Pasta Carbonara 173

    Mac 'n' Tease 174

    Pasta Salad with Curry Dressing 175

    Beet Wellington 176

Problems with Popular Plants 178

Chapter 10—Zero Waste on the Go **181**

Make Your Own Zero-Waste Kit 182

Sustainable Vacations 184

    Great vacations without planes 185

    Buying green while on vacation 189

Chapter 11—Waste Free for Parties and Holidays **193**

Gifts 195

    The homemade 196

    The pre-loved 196

    The experience 198

Gift Wrapping 198

    Do like Grandma 199

    Refuse gift wrapping 199

    Use what you already have 199

Chapter 12—Plastic-Free Care Products **201**

Oral Hygiene 202

Shaving 203

Soap Guide 204

    A solid soap tip 206

Periods 206

DIY Makeup and Beauty Tips 207

    Homemade Body Lotion 210

    Homemade Setting Powder 212

    Homemade Concealer 212

    Homemade Blush 213

    Homemade Lip Tint 214

    Homemade Eyebrow Tint/Eye Shadow 216

    Homemade Mascara 217

    Easy Facemask 217

    Charcoal Mask 218

Products That You Might Want to Phase Out or
Stop Buying Right Away 221

Chapter 13—I Am Super Green—Now What? **227**

Chapter 14—Guilt Does Not Plant Trees **229**

Works Cited and Sources 238

Special Thanks 243

About the Author 244

Foreword

The past few years have seen some of the worst environmental disasters in history, signaling a new era of accelerating environmental destabilization. Food security and the strength of our global systems to meet basic human needs are under threat and have already caused irreparable damage in the Global South. As our levels of consumption increase, so do the demands for fossil fuels and cheap labor. This is wholly unsustainable, and without systemic change, we cannot turn the tide on environmental destruction.

All that said, there has been a fundamental shift in the perception of how the climate and waste crises are being handled. And with the advanced scrutiny coming from creators like Gittemarie, young activists living on the frontlines of climate change, and organizations, there is hope for our future.

Many have argued that individual action cannot save the planet, but to the contrary, many individuals have galvanized the world into action. However, we mustn't look to one person to motivate us, to see the enormity of the problem we are facing. Instead, we should individually do our parts and come together to create an even greater voice.

Individual action plants a seed of hope in every single person who makes one swap, one lifestyle change, or reads one book outside their comfort zone. It is this action that helps to shift our mindset from overconsumption to mindful consumption, from buying the latest and greatest to choosing second-hand and vintage. While our one swap at a time may not immediately change the world, those around us will see our actions and may make one swap of their own.

When you get thousands if not millions of individuals looking inward at their own actions, you get thousands of potential comrades with which to join forces. That self-scrutiny paves the way to create curious minds in all of us. If I want to stop consuming so many vegetables in plastic packaging, I may think about where I could shop to do so. After a time, I may consider how the shops themselves could make consumers' lives easier by offering unpackaged foods. Eventually, this may lead me to ask, "Why is so much plastic packaging used and how could policy affect the whole country's level of consumption?" And then, it may lead to collective action, to protest, to petition, to actual systemic change.

Gittemarie is particularly well-qualified, personally and professionally, to contribute to this conversation, and many of us who have followed her for years have learned a tremendous amount. One aspect of her work that is much needed is her in-depth video content that interrogates the validity of many sustainable claims. As an individual it is often difficult to decipher what is and isn't greenwashing. Many brands seeking to offer consumers a more sustainable option often use buzzwords that actually lead to more confusion. I have no doubt that you will gain the tools needed to live more sustainably at the end of this book, and hopefully, it will motivate you to join forces and be a part of a collective for a more sustainable future.

Imogen "Immy" Lucas
Sustainablility/low-impact blogger and
influencer (@sustainably_vegan)

Preface

In January of 2015, I began an experiment. I wanted to live without producing any trash for a month. I had never been interested in sustainability before, and I had no idea where to begin, but I just threw myself into it headfirst. Through my experience with zero waste, I have learned that if we want to live in a more sustainable society, there are no shortcuts and easy fixes. At least, this the case if we want to permanently implement the green agenda into our daily lives. There are hundreds of ways to change your habits but, like with every other lifestyle change, they require patience and commitment. We live in a world where convenience and luxury dictate many consumers' priorities and where most companies would rather sell us products that make us sick and unhappy than create a positive impact.

Wow, okay, that sounds super woke, and maybe a little too holier-than-thou-ish for most tastes, but honestly, that is how it is. For that reason, it can be difficult to navigate all the information and all the noise which is affecting the discourse of sustainability. In this noise, it's super difficult to figure out what is right and what is wrong and whether trying to live sustainably even matters if we cannot do it perfectly. At least, those were my thoughts five years ago.

As consumers and citizens of the world, we are often told that we can never change anything alone, that we are forced to sit down and wait for companies and politicians to get their act together and then include us in their green agenda when they are ready to do so. But as an individual consumer, you can change a whole lot by yourself simply by changing your habits—where you shop, what you buy, and what you choose not to buy all have an important role to play. Because every time we pay for a product, we vote. We vote for what kind of future we want. I am hopeful that this book will make it easier for you to live a more sustainable life. Actually, my hope is that this book will give you an idea of what changes are effective, where the most meaningful changes happen, and how it's all connected.

There are millions of sustainable lifestyles and there is no one true answer which can explain all that is right and all that is wrong. Okay, maybe there are some answers, but, because we are different and because we all have different lives and needs, the question "What is most sustainable?" doesn't always have a consistent answer.

Maybe this is not exactly the most constructive and helpful way to start writing a book about sustainability, but that is how life is sometimes. I think it's better to be aware of the adversities one might face before jumping in. But no matter how different our lives may be, there are some things that are good to know as a consumer. Some things that we consume in our everyday lives are just not ideal, or even remotely up to par, which is not necessarily our fault, so the companies that are benefitting from our consumption of these goods need to get it together. And on that note, it is time for a disclaimer (of sorts). I want to thoroughly highlight that all the steps we take toward being more sustainable are valid; more importantly, not everyone takes the same steps, and all routes to sustainability are valid. Sustainability rarely comes in one-size-fits-all, and while I might highlight some habits and actions that I was able to change, or that I benefitted from changing, it might be different for you. This is where I want you to remember that it is okay if your sustainability journey does not look exactly like mine, it's just as good. I have based this book in my own experiences of life, and as such, the habits and actions that I have chosen to include reflect those I have experienced myself. I want you to remember that it might not be universally applicable in every situation; that would simply be impossible (or at least make the book so heavy that no one would be able to pick it up). You might not be in a position where you are able to make similar decisions or cut out certain products right now, or ever. I want you to remember that even trying is a bloody amazing thing; just picking up a book to learn more about sustainability is more than many people do, so you're already on a good track. I want you to remember this if you ever feel discouraged or like you are not enough. We are all just trying our best.

So, this book is partly a lifestyle guide for those who want to live a greener life and who want to know how the heck one might actually do that. But it is also a book that explains some of the issues with our everyday products. This book is filled with personal anecdotes from my own journey, from being a shopping connoisseur and a hyper-consumer to a zero waster. Additionally, it also has tons of facts that might come in handy and that will hopefully give you a bit of an overview. So here you go: use *Sustainable Badass* as a lifestyle guide, a work of reference, a collection of recipes, and/or as pages to guide you through daily dilemmas when it is unclear what to do. You are of course always free to do whatever you want, but if you want to be a sustainable badass, it always helps to have done your homework first.

—*Gittemarie Johansen*

Chapter 1
THE PLASTIC PROBLEM

The first time I ever noticed the term "zero waste" was in an article about a woman from New York who could fit all her trash of three years into a single mason jar. I thought that sounded fascinating because I was making more trash than that just during an average day. That article started something in me, because I had never actually thought about my trash and where it ends up. Okay, I knew that it, of course, did not just disappear into thin air but that the trash pickup would take care of it and send it off to a local waste plant—so far so good. But I paid very little attention to my trash, and because of this, it felt like stepping into a completely new world when I started to find out what the problems with plastic actually are. So, I think it's only fitting that this book will start in the same place that I started my own journey toward sustainability, and that is with the plastic problem.

This Is How Plastic Is Made

Every piece of plastic that has ever been produced in human history still exists in some shape or form. This was the first thing I learned about plastic when I started to seek out information about sustainability and pollution back in January of 2015, and that fact has resonated in my mind ever since. Regardless of how plastic is managed, once it has been thrown away, it will never disappear. Ninety percent of global plastic produced is based on fossil materials. In contrast to other materials like cardboard or paper, plastic will never decompose; it will only be reduced to smaller pieces of plastic. As a result, even in countries or areas where waste is burned in incinerator plants, it won't disappear into thin air. The plastic merely changes its shape but remains as resistant to decomposition as ever. But before we venture into a discussion of why plastic is bad and, more importantly, what we can do differently, we have to talk about what plastic actually is.

The cheapest way to produce plastic is through *fracking*, a process which retrieves crude oil from underground. The primary goal of this process is to extract oil for fuel production. However, a byproduct from this process is the greenhouse gas ethane. After the extraction, this gas is converted into ethylene through a process called *cracking*, and that is what plastic is made of. The process of fracking is extremely polluting and harmful for many reasons, one of them being the methane emissions it produces. This greenhouse gas is 25 percent more potent than CO_2. From here, it does not take a lot of effort to get to the conclusion that the production of plastic has a harmful effect on our planet. Plastic production emits methane. It then requires energy and transportation to distribute the plastic, and we ultimately throw it away without a second thought (even though it's here forever). That is not exactly a perfect combination.

So why do we use that crap? There are, of course, many answers to that question, but a good place to start is with the industry that produces it. When I had to do research for my very first lecture about zero-waste living, I ran an internet search that went something like "What the heck is plastic actually made of?" because, truthfully, I did not actually know. One of the first results that came up was an article published by a representative of the European plastic industry (something I did not initially realize). I clicked on the article, and it said that plastic is an organic material like paper and wool. Everything about this article made plastic sound like a natural product that our modern civilization gladly could use without any worry.

I learned a very important lesson here: While we as consumers are willing to inform ourselves and be critical toward the products we use every day, the industries that make those products are lying in wait to misinform and mislead us. These companies have made it unbelievably difficult to navigate what is true and what is false. I guess that companies producing plastic products are not exactly jumping with joy over the fact that plastic is facing more criticism than ever before. So they invest massive amounts of financial resources, trying to keep our focus away from the fact that the product they produce has a devastating effect on the planet.

There is a lot to take in and a lot to change, but a good place to start is by minimizing our use of plastic and especially single-use plastic.

Facts about plastic

- A plastic product is used for an average of twelve minutes before it is discarded.

- Fifty percent of all plastic is only used once before it is thrown away.

- Forty percent of all plastic is produced for packaging.

- An average American throws away roughly 286 pounds of plastic every year.

Microplastic

So what happens to plastic once it degrades? Microplastics are small plastic particles that are smaller than ¼ inch across, and they are a result of plastic that degrades. As mentioned before, plastic does not technically decompose, it just becomes smaller pieces of plastic—a.k.a. microplastic. These particles are often so small that they cannot be filtered through water and sewage treatment plants, and as a result, they end up in rivers, lakes, oceans, and yes, even in our own tap water.

A study from Medical University of Vienna found microplastic in the stomachs of eight different people from eight different countries. We all ingest microplastic in the form of regular consumer products like our food and drink. However, an especially high concentration of microplastic has been found in many animal products like fish, shellfish, and honey. Although, it's not only with food products that we should be aware of microplastic. Car tires generate particularly high amounts of microplastic, and a large amount of the microplastic generated by the average person comes from this source. As some of you may have guessed, this is because car tires are made with plastic components and the material is worn down on the asphalt.

Synthetic materials also have a role to play here. Every time we use or wash a piece of synthetic clothing, like a polyester shirt or a microfiber washcloth, microplastic is released from the material. A shirt or a cloth is basically worn down in the same way as car tires. Another big player in the microplastic discharge game is beauty and care products; products like face and body scrubs, toothpaste, makeup, and, of course, glitter. (Later in this book, we will get back to what types of microplastic there are and how to avoid them.) However, I want to add that several restrictions and laws, especially in Europe, have been put in place in order to combat unnecessary microplastic in things like beauty and care products. Even so, microplastic in the products you buy is always a good thing to be aware of, especially as an American consumer. Overall, there are still tons of improvements we, as well as our governments, can make to combat microplastic.

Garbage Islands

It seems unlikely that all microplastic in the oceans comes from car tires and polyester shirts, right? Well, that's because this is not true. The majority of plastic particles in the world's oceans, which are ingested by humans and animals through water and food, come from plastic dumped in nature. When plastic is left in direct sunlight or in water, it will start degrading into smaller particles because the material becomes worn down and weakened. It simply falls apart. Perhaps you know those really old plastic food containers from your grandparents' house? You know, the one that's so soft that the lid will not fit on the top of the container anymore? This is actually the same thing that happens to plastic when it is worn down by nature, only it tends to happen quicker because the conditions are constant and the scale of the weakening of plastic is much larger in nature than in your grandparents' pantry.

Plastic can end up in our oceans in a lot of different ways: wind can carry it out of an open-lid bin and fly it to the beach; birds or other animals can transport it long distances; people can drop it on streets and in public places; and, sometimes, plastic is left in nature on purpose. It is estimated that a truckload's worth of plastic trash is dumped in our oceans every second, and that has serious consequences. A 2018 study from the European Parliament estimated that there is approximately 150 million metric tons of plastic in the ocean today; a number which is only increasing because every year an additional eight million metric tons of plastic ends up at sea.

In some countries, the majority of consumer waste is burned at waste-to-energy incinerator plants, and in those cases, it can be hard to see how that waste plays any part in ocean pollution. Even if most waste is burned, it's still a massive problem. With increasing consumer waste, most waste plants cannot manage all the trash we produce, and as a result, waste is sold and shipped to other places in the world. Even countries that talk a big game about not using open landfills occasionally get around that by shipping waste out of the country to, for example, Poland or Malaysia, where the waste will eventually end up in a landfill anyway. As a result of this "trash export," certain areas don't have the capacity to properly manage or handle the increasing amounts that are expected of them. An example of this is China, which in 2017 ceased its import of American waste. The burden of both local and Western waste can also be seen in India, Bangladesh, Indonesia, and Malaysia. These countries are used by Western companies for cheap, outsourced production of goods due to less-strict environmental requirements and laws, leaving these areas with not only the waste and production of their own population but much of the burden of Western consumerism as well.

When truck after truck dumps plastic waste in the ocean, that plastic is going to gather on the surface of the water, because most plastic floats. It then gathers in bundles because the world's oceans are connected by currents—the same currents which are an essential part of our tempered climate. Those currents distribute and transport warm and cold water, but they also work kind of like a centrifuge for the waste that floats on top. There are multiple garbage islands in the world, but the largest one goes by the name the Great Pacific Garbage Patch and is located—yeah, this is pretty self-explanatory—in the Pacific Ocean. This island of waste weighs in at around 95,900 tons and takes up an area that is twice the size of Texas. It is 618,000 square miles and is made of more than 1.8 billion pieces of plastic from all over the world.

But what is the garbage island made of? Several studies show that the Great Pacific Garbage Patch contains daily consumer waste from all over the world. The plastic packaging from that ice cream you had at the beach last summer can actually end up as part of a trash island or float up on a coast halfway around the globe. However, it is not only daily consumer waste that constitutes the garbage islands. Fishnets and other fishing gear make up the largest uniform category of waste in the oceans today, with 705 tons of gear, nets, traps, and lines which are left behind by the fishing industry every year; this is also called *ghost gear*. A mixed group of different daily consumer products makes up 49 percent of all plastic in the oceans.

The ten largest categories of consumer products in the ocean, according to a study by the EU, are:

1. Water bottles, lids, and caps
2. Cigarette butts
3. Cotton swabs
4. Candy wrapper and snack bags
5. Hygiene products like tampons, pads, and insertion sleeves
6. Plastic bags
7. Single-use cutlery and straws
8. Plastic cups and lids
9. Balloons and balloon sticks
10. Plastic containers like fast-food packaging

What Are We Doing about It?

When you read all these facts, it is easy to feel a little alone in the world and alone with all your worries. But you're certainly not alone. Luckily, several countries and communities have already taken great steps to ban or restrict certain types of plastic to combat the waste problem. In 2017, Kenya restricted plastic bags and introduced the world's strictest laws against plastic pollution. In the same year, Vanuatu, as the first island in the Pacific, began a plastic ban which would restrict the use of plastic bags and bottles. In the beginning of 2018, England announced a twenty-five-year plan that will remove microplastic from beauty products, as well as a restriction on cotton swabs, straws, and plastic bottles. In 2019, Taiwan began a long-term project that will ensure an efficient recycling process as well as a gradual ban on straws, cutlery, cups, and bags made from single-use plastic. In 2017, Zimbabwe announced a complete ban on the plastic product EPS, which is a type of packaging that resembles polystyrene and that can neither decompose nor be recycled. Furthermore, several countries have introduced, or talked about introducing, fees and taxes on plastic bags, though there are no countries that match the efforts of Rwanda. Since 2008, Rwanda has had a complete ban on plastic bags, a ban so strictly enforced that it may result in a prison sentence if ignored. According to the organization Plastic Oceans, Rwanda is working toward being completely plastic free in the near future. There are several other places in the world where we are also seeing improvements on, and restriction of, the use of plastic: political green action in Denmark is introducing an expanded return system for plastic bottles and cans as well as a ban on some plastic bags and an efficient recycling system. ("An efficient recycling system" is something that is commonly spoken of in the context of sustainable political action.) Recycling is often regarded as the best method with which to combat the waste issue, but how exactly is plastic recycled?

Chapter 2

Recycling: A Waste-Management Guide

It is difficult to create an everyday routine wherein everything you encounter comes completely without packaging. In an average day, you will most likely come in contact with packaging and other products with limited life spans, and that will generate waste. The expression "zero waste" can therefore easily be misleading, because many people will hear it and instantly think that the person using this expression creates absolutely no waste, zero, nada—as the name so cleverly suggests. But in reality, the name refers to a general goal rather than the actual practice. To produce absolutely zero waste, one would have to be in control of every aspect of one's life, including what guests, friends, and family bring into your home or what is put in your hand at work, in school, at the gym, or at any other location. Of course, it is possible to refuse tons of items, but we most likely will generate small amounts of waste, even when we try not to. Therefore, this chapter includes a recycling guide that will go over some of the different materials we surround ourselves with, what the heck they are, how they are produced, how we should sort them, and what advantages (and disadvantages) they each present us with. Personally, I think that the zero-waste lifestyle is about throwing away as little as possible, even if it is sorted for recycling. I don't want to use the refusal of plastic as a "get-out-of-jail-free card" to use other materials like glass, metal, or cardboard mindlessly. On the contrary, it is better to minimize the amount of all types of single-use packaging and disposable products in general. But again, it is close to impossible to produce no waste at all, so here is a guide on how to navigate, and stay critical of, recycling.

How Is Plastic Recycled?

When plastic is recycled, it must be sorted into categories based on what type of plastic it is, because different types of plastic cannot always be recycled together. That is why many products made from a mix of several types of plastic are completely unrecyclable and will simply be sorted as waste for incineration or landfill depending on the area, region, or country. You can always recognize the different types of plastic by looking at the triangle imprint typically found at the bottom of the product (often it surrounds a number or a letter as well). This will tell you which type of plastic you're dealing with. Furthermore, some types of plastic are generally recognized to be safer for use than others, and because of this, it is a good idea to know a little bit about the effects of the plastic, as well as what the markings on the plastic indicate. Some types of plastic contain stuff like BPA, or bisphenol A, a component that has been shown to have hormone-disruptive effects in humans. Studies have been conducted that show BPA can have a negative effect on the quality of sperm and cause premature puberty symptoms in children. This is partly because the concentration of BPA is rather high in many toys, reusable plastic water bottles, lunchboxes, and other plastic products that you put in your mouth—come to think of it, there are quite a lot of those products.

- **PET (1)** is used to make soft plastic bottles for water, juice, or cooking oil. PET does not contain BPA, but if the material is left out in the sunlight it can release antimony, a moderately toxic metalloid, which is absorbed in liquid and can irritate the stomach and large intestines.

- **HDPE (2)** is used as packaging for cleaning products, shampoo bottles, and foils. Generally described as safe by the plastic industry, some studies show that if it is exposed to lots of direct sunlight or heat, HDPE can release substances that imitate estrogen.

- **PVC (3)** is used in construction and for pipes and plumbing, but it can also be found in packaging. PVC contains phthalates, which are softening components that have been shown to be highly hormone disruptive and can affect testosterone production.

- **LDPE (4)** is used for plastic shopping bags and often for packaging as well. This type of plastic does not contain BPA either, but just like HDPE it can release substances that imitate estrogen.

- **PP (5)** is often used in furniture and suitcases, as well as in cars and toys. This type of plastic generally poses no harm when exposed to heat and does not release toxins as many other types of plastic might.

- **PS (6)** is also used in toy production, as well as for hard packaging like DVD cases or containers for cosmetics. PS is also known as polystyrene and can be made into soft plastic foam. Under influence of high temperatures, PS will release styrene, which is a known carcinogen.

- **Other (7):** The last category includes stuff like fiberglass, nylon, and polycarbonate. These types of plastic are used to make everything from CDs to baby bottles. Studies have found that this category generally releases both BPA and other hormone disruptors and is connected to type 2 diabetes and heart disease.

When the differently sorted plastics have been divided correctly, they're cut into smaller pieces, then infrared technology will again sort the plastic so that the materials are left as clean as possible.

Afterward, they are cut into even smaller pieces. The plastic bits are melted into plastic pellets that can be used for new products. According to representatives of the Danish plastic industry, most recycled plastic pellets are made into new packaging or plastic shopping bags. They can also be repurposed as a synthetic textile or synthetic filling for sleeping bags. Most plastic, when recycled, is often *downcycled* to less useful or otherwise unrecyclable products like fillings or thin and soft packaging. That is because plastic cannot be recycled indefinitely. After merely two to three recycling circles, new plastic must be added to the plastic pellets to maintain the material's desired quality level. Therefore, plastic cannot function in a closed system or a circular economy because new, virgin plastic would have to be continuously added in the process of recycling.

So the use, or misuse, of plastic can rarely be justified by recycling. This is especially true for everyday products and packaging, which could easily be avoided for most people, as the recycling system is nowhere near efficient enough to meet global, or even local, demand. The global recycling rate for plastic is around 9–12 percent, and even higher rates rarely exceed 30 percent.

However, it is extremely important that we use the plastic we have already produced, and which can be found in nature and in the oceans. This plastic should be collected and utilized in ways that will ensure that it will not end up as litter again. One way of doing this would be through innovation in the construction industry. There are also clothing brands that incorporate plastic materials in their textile production, a concept which comes with its own disadvantages (which I would also like to critically address, but we are going to talk about that in the textile chapter).

What about Bioplastic?

Bioplastic, in contrast to ordinary plastic, is made from plant-based sources like corn, straw, beets, sugarcane, or bamboo. Bioplastic can be used like ordinary petroleum-based plastic to make packaging, bottles, foil, and other plastic products. An advantage of bioplastic is that, when it starts to degrade, it will not emit more CO_2 than the plants the bioplastic is made from absorbed while they were growing. So the amount of CO_2 bioplastic emits is equivalent to the amount the plants involved previously absorbed—making the bioplastic CO_2 neutral! (If the material is made 100 percent from plants, that is.) As we know, ordinary plastic emits both CO_2 and methane which was previously stored in crude oil. Petroleum-based plastic is made of fossil materials which would normally not be found in an above-ground environment and will therefore always add negatively to global emissions. About 1 percent of all plastic comes from bioplastic production, and today the material is most frequently used to make single-use products like straws, plastic bags, packaging for fast food, or as to-go packaging.

Another advantage of bioplastic is that it can be produced anywhere in the world. In contrast, crude oil is abundant in certain places but not everywhere. Because of this, bioplastic would create workplaces and profitable business in areas and countries that need it. On the other hand, the growing demand for bioplastic may cause certain areas to transform their fields and agriculture from food products to plant products for bioplastic production. The rising demand for bioplastic isn't solely a positive one, as many countries produce the plant material for its production while they also battle poverty and hunger. Another disadvantage of bioplastic is that it is a fairly new product and it requires specialized recycling facilities to break it down—as bioplastic isn't biodegradable in nature or in a home compost. It requires a controlled environment to break it down, and if it is left in nature it will take years to degrade. There are very few bioplastic recycling facilities as of this moment, and therefore, bioplastic is often burned or ends up in landfills.

Bioplastic is, however, better than normal petroleum-based plastic because it emits less CO_2 during its decomposition or incineration, but unfortunately it is rarely recycled or repurposed. Bioplastic can also complicate the recycling of normal plastic if the materials are mixed. There are many products that are made of a mix between normal plastic and bioplastic, and these products cannot be recycled at all. So, clearly, bioplastic is a tough nut to crack. There are countless types of "green" plastic that are often called bioplastic, but you might also encounter "compostable" plastic, "plant-based" plastic, or "naturally green" plastic. As a result, it is incredibly difficult to make general claims about the abilities of bioplastic because these products vary so much in quality and ability. Some products can be 100 percent plant based and can sometimes be composted at home, whereas others will act completely like normal plastic and never biodegrade outside a specialized facility.

All in all, this field is super difficult for the consumer to navigate, and it can be just as difficult to determine whether a bioplastic product is actually sustainable or not. My advice is if the company can prove that their product is compostable, then go for it, but if not, it's better to keep those products at a distance. Bioplastic is, as mentioned, primarily used to make single-use products, and more often than not it is better to avoid disposables altogether because a reusable alternative is always more sustainable.

In 2019, I was in a restaurant in Copenhagen and was about to order lunch. I have made it a habit of mine to always specify while ordering: "Oh and by the way, hold the straw please. I don't need it." Often, I even say this before specifying which drink I want, simply so the staff remember it better. The waiter, who was incredibly kind and helpful,

told me that I did not have to worry about the impact of straws, or the
turtles and all that, because their straws were made of compostable
plastic. That sounded great, so, impressed as I was, I asked if they
composted their waste. They did not, and, honestly, I think the waiter
was a little confused about my relationship with plastic. I simply
said, as politely as possible, that I would still like to avoid the straw.
A product with compostable qualities is only going to have a positive
impact if it is actually composted, otherwise it simply goes the same
place as all the other waste.

How Is Organic Waste Recycled?

Organic waste covers the large category of waste that is
compostable, such as food waste. To recycle or repurpose the
organic waste, it is transformed into *bio-pulp*. This is a uniform
substance that is created by tightly pressing the organic material in
specialized facilities. The end result can be repurposed as fertilizer.
The advantage of this type of waste management is that it emits
less CO_2 and methane than fertilizer from animals (a.k.a. manure).
The reason for this is that organic waste ideally can consist primarily
of plant-based materials, like veggie scraps and plants, which emit
less greenhouse gases than animal products—this is true for both
production and disposal.

Organic waste can also be used to produce bio-gas, another process
that has some advantages. First of all, bio-gas can be stored and used
at a later point in time, whereas the energy that is released when
incinerating waste cannot be stored and has to be used right away—
so bio-gas production wastes a lot less energy. The energy from bio-
gas can be used to produce fuel for public transportation (shout-out
of appreciation to the bio-buses in my hometown of Aalborg!). But
there are also disadvantages when it comes to bio-gas, and here I am
not talking about the frequently heard, "Urgh, but the facilities are

so ugly to look at." Heck, if a waste plant can reduce emissions and help save the planet, you can build it in my living room for all I care. However, there are other, and slightly more serious, disadvantages. This is actually related to the content of organic waste used for this purpose. In contrast to composting, bio-gas production can involve animal products like meat, bones, and processed products—you don't want to add those items to your compost, but they're allowed in organic recycling because a large part of bio-gas already comes from animal sources. The bio-gas we can produce from organic waste functions as a supplement to an already existing energy source. Bio-gas is already made with manure from animal agriculture. Using animal-based organic waste as a fertilizer has a substantial and negative effect on groundwater reserves, and it emits tons of methane as well. Globally, we're experiencing oxygen depletion in both large and small bodies of water, and this is partly due to the heavy use of fertilizer from animals. Oxygen depletion makes it impossible for most animals and small organisms to live in the water, which means that this issue is directly related to loss of biodiversity. If you want to know more about composting, you can pop over to the compost guide in Chapter 5.

How Is Glass Recycled?

Glass, like plastic, cannot break down in nature. However, it can be recycled indefinitely without losing quality or structure. Glass can be collected as intact bottles or containers which will be cleaned and used again, or, if the glass is broken, it can be melted into new glass products. There are also several types of glass products (and other fragile materials) that cannot be recycled, like ceramics and lightbulbs, as these can cause problems during recycling. (It is again important for me to note that the requirements and options for recycling might vary greatly from country to country, so always reach out to your local recycling stations and find out the specifics for your area.) When you are sorting glass, you have to empty the containers. Some recycling companies state that you don't have to clean them completely before sorting but, again, this may vary. You can also repurpose glass packaging at home and use it as storage containers for leftovers or for bulk shopping. Glass is a good alternative to plastic for storage of food because glass will not release toxic chemicals when exposed to sunlight or heat, as many types of plastic will. The production of new glass has an environmental impact of 0.91 kg CO_2, whereas the recycling process for one pound of glass has an impact of circa 0.28 kg of CO_2. Likewise, the emission related to material consumption when producing one pound of new glass, is 0.5 kg CO_2, whereas the recycling of one pound of glass is 0 kg CO_2—because no new material has to be added to the process. These numbers, as well as the upcoming ones in this chapter, have been published by the Danish Environmental Protection Agency, however, the studies don't include transportation emissions.

One of the reasons why it is more sustainable to recycle glass than to produce it new is because they are two vastly different processes which require vastly different temperatures. To produce new glass products, you need a core temperature of 2,700 degrees Fahrenheit. It requires a lot of energy to keep those temperatures up, and furthermore, when a glass furnace is hot and running, it is not going to cool down until the day it is out of business. It simply requires too much energy to reach such a high temperature. Conversely, simply recycling and remelting glass requires much lower temperatures. It is even better if the glass products don't have to be remelted but can simply be cleaned and shipped out to refill.

How Is Paper Recycled?

Paper and cardboard can only be recycled somewhere between seven and ten times, and they degrade slightly in quality every time they are recycled. Paper that has not been recycled many times before can easily become new white paper—however, the more times paper and cardboard are recycled, the more difficult it will be to pull ink, glue, and surface treatments out of the paper material. Most recycled paper will end its life as newspapers, eggs trays, and wallpaper. Paper is made from long fibers, and for every time it is recycled, the fibers are shortened; in the end, the fibers will not be long enough to produce normal sheets of paper. When the fibers are too short, they will be mixed with new fibers and the paper can no longer be classified as a recycled product. You can also encounter paper products that many recycling facilities will not accept and which thus cannot be recycled in some cases—these are products that, like plastic, are made from mixed materials. Cartons such as food packaging for milk and juice, for instance, can only be recycled in a few countries. In the case of this type of packaging, which is called Tetra Pak, the paper and cardboard fibers are mixed with plastic, and many recycling stations don't have the technology to take it apart. Again, what is accepted for recycling and what is not may vary greatly, and this is also true for paper. Some recycling systems will pick up paper trash from each individual household, whereas other systems require you to drop your paper recycling off yourself. When paper and cardboard are recycled, they have to be dry and clean. Because of this, cardboard products like pizza boxes with grease stains cannot be recycled. I recommend cutting out the stains and composting those while sorting all the clean parts of the pizza box. Producing one pound of new paper has an impact of about 0.7 kg CO_2, whereas recycling only requires circa. 0.32 kg. Likewise, the production of one pound of new paper requires six gallons of water, whereas recycling one pound only requires circa six kgs.

How Is Metal Recycled?

Metals like aluminum fall into the category of materials that, when recycled correctly, can be reused indefinitely without losing structure or quality. Actually, around 75 percent of all the aluminum ever produced is still in use today. When metal is collected for recycling, it is remelted, but even if that process requires a fair amount of resources (it always does when high temperatures and melting are involved), it has a significantly lower impact than producing new metal. The production of new metal is contributing to the loss of the rainforest and relies on unethical mining. If metal is not recycled but instead sorted with non-recyclable waste, it will either end up in a landfill or in an incinerator, which can cause big problems for the facilities because it will melt and get stuck in the machinery. The production of one pound of iron or steel will have an impact of 1.6 kg of CO_2, whereas recycling will only have an impact of about 0.15 kg. Likewise, producing one pound of aluminum has an impact of circa 6 kg of CO_2, however recycling one pound only emits 0.4 kg—so merely 5 percent of the impact of producing new material. Furthermore, BPA is also found in some aluminum products like tins and cans. Here, the inside part of the packaging is covered with a soft plastic component which in many cases may contain BPA. However, many countries are starting to pass bans on the use of plastic softeners that contain BPA, especially those found in tins and receipts. In Europe, 39 percent of the aluminum produced is used for vehicles and transport such as cars, planes, trucks, and buses, as wells as bikes. Furthermore, 24 percent of aluminum is used in the construction industry. Although we also use a fair share in the production of household appliances, it is unfortunately not always recycled. A European citizen uses an average of forty-eight pounds of aluminum products in a year, and that consumption primarily involves soda cans, tins, aluminum foil, and single-use packaging.

The two last categories especially are often thrown away with non-recyclable waste—even though the material can be recycled forever.

What about Return Systems?

Effective return systems can be much more sustainable than curbside recycling: every time you buy a beverage you are paying a small amount more than the product's actual price, but you will get that money back once you return the packaging. All bottles and cans have the extra fee, and they can be returned in practically every supermarket. In contrast to other types of recycling, most packaging in this return system is recycled in a closed loop, with more cleaning and refilling and less remelting. Generally, there are two types of recycling systems—open and closed. In an open system, the material is produced and processed so that it can be turned into new and different products. Whereas in a closed system the material is processed in order to be reused as what it already is—for instance, a glass bottle will be shipped out as a glass bottle again. In the Danish return system, the recycle rate of bottles and cans is at 90 percent, and is thus much higher than the general recycling rate for both plastic and metals. But can we just consume all the packaging if it is included in a return system and freely use plastic with a good conscience? No. The impact of recycled products is lower than that of producing new ones, but the best solution is still to minimize waste, as plastic cannot be recycled forever in the return system.

I once brought a case of beers for a garden party, and one of the beers looked slightly different from the rest. It was a bottle that originally had belonged to the brand Chang Beer, and the bottle itself had a Buddha engraved on the side, but a Carlsberg label was glued on top—and the contents of the bottles also belonged to Carlsberg. I thought it was a super fun oddity, and we ended up saving the bottle. I think one of my friends still has it. I also think it is a perfect example of how the return system recycles glass bottles in a closed loop. I have also once been served a beer at a bar in a glass bottle that had "John" carved on the bottom, with, I am guessing, a key or another sharp object. It was definitely not standard factory design. Because the glass bottles are not remelted but rather cleaned and refilled, no one had noticed or done anything about it. I think it is a nice example of how glass can be refilled over and over again.

Recycling is a practice that has both advantages and disadvantages, but seen through a lens of sustainability, we generate way too much waste, regardless of whether it is recycled or not. Many countries and regions turn their waste into energy at neatly named waste-to-energy-plants rather than relying on landfills for waste storage. The advantage of doing this is that we don't have to import as much crude oil for the production of heat and energy. Instead, we can use the energy stored in waste that we have already produced. But the problem with plastic will not disappear, not even when it is incinerated. Instead, the plastic becomes small particles—fumes and ashes—which luckily are caught in filters above the incinerator to avoid them polluting the air. But those filters will become a waste product of their own, and a toxic one at that. They will be burned themselves, or buried underground, and sometimes they are incorporated into building materials.

It is difficult to find a facility that incinerates waste and wants to talk about what happens to those filters, but in 2018 I gave a lecture about zero waste at a waste-to-energy incinerator plant, and I got to ask the staff what happens to the filters. From what I gathered from their answers, the filters are most often just buried underground. Even in countries that don't use open landfills as a waste-management solution, waste is still frequently buried underground. The types of trash that end up like that are products that generally cannot be recycled or burned—stuff like large kitchen appliances, polluted soil, soft PVC plastic, and asbestos. To dispose of those products, we dig a large hole in the ground, fill it with toxic waste, and cover it with soil, which is far from a perfect solution. Over the years, I have realized that perfect solutions, when it comes to waste management, are sparse. But there is a solution that is not necessarily *easy* so much as it is *simple*—simply produce less waste.

Chapter 3

Going Green: Working Toward Zero Waste

The zero-waste lifestyle utilizes a set of principles that focuses on waste prevention as a primary goal. It is a concept that originates from production and factory terminology, and it refers to a production line with no waste product. The zero-waste principles are based on a circular system in which as little as possible is wasted. The principles are explained rather nicely by understanding "the five Rs" in a hierarchical order. (This overview can be found in many sources that talk about zero-waste living, however I have chosen to add a sixth point.)

Refuse: Say no and avoiding certain products based on their packaging, impact, or production.

Reduce: If we cannot refuse all together, we can lessen our consumption, especially of things we do not have any essential use for.

Reuse: Use products over and over rather than buying new things, or if you're in need of something new, buy it secondhand.

Recycle: Actively sort and recycle the waste you do produce so the resources are not wasted on one product.

Rot: Let appropriate products decompose, or use a compost to create a circular system.

Repair (my own addition): Fix and maintain the things you own to avoid buying new things or throwing out unnecessary amounts.

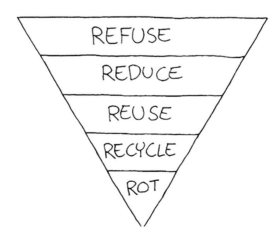

How I Got Started

During the winter of 2015, I was looking through an article about plastic, completely by coincidence. I had just started my studies at Aalborg University, and I was sitting in my very first studio apartment—one of the good ones where you straight-up cook dinner and sleep in the same room. The article was about the previously mentioned woman in Chapter 1 who could fit three years of trash into a mason jar, and the headline read something like: "Every Piece of Plastic We Have Ever Produced Still Exists" (extra, extra, read all about it!). Upon reading it, my body felt heavy and sad. I had seriously never thought about my trash, so it seemed almost uncomfortable to watch someone display and exhibit it. I had always had this relationship with trash, and I think a lot of others have had it as well, and in that specific moment, I was suddenly confronted with this relationship that I never even thought enough about to define, let alone change. Every time I threw something away, in either a public or a private bin, my ownership of that trash would cease. It was no longer my property once it left my hand and landed in a bin. I have already known that you're not allowed to litter in nature or on the street, and that it's my responsibility to throw my trash away. But once the trash was in the bin, my job was done, and I had done well because, after all, that is where trash belongs.

When I saw this trash jar, it forced me to redefine my relationship with waste. It started this avalanche of change in my life. Firstly, I began looking differently at waste and what I was throwing away. I also started mentally taking note of every piece of trash I generated. The trash started to mean something. It did not feel forced or like something I had to do—I simply could not help it. After this, I started going through my own bin, which is probably one of the most uncomfortable things I have ever done—yeah, bins are gross, y'all. But I was so curious and driven to change, so there I was, sitting on the floor of my studio apartment, completely covered in trash as I tried to map out my consumer habits like I was a sailor lost at sea. I guess I looked weird, (actually, I am not guessing, I most certainly did), but I learned a whole lot about what I was throwing away. Next, I started thinking about solutions and alternatives to the waste in my bin (or on the floor, more like it). I knew I would be able to avoid aluminum foil by using a lunchbox, and that would also save me a plastic bag. The same went for leftovers, which I would also previously have individually wrapped in plastic or foil. And I could avoid small plastic bags by bringing my own bags to the supermarket when grocery shopping. This train of thought went on for a really long time. I decided to try to live a completely zero-waste lifestyle for a month. Yep, a month. I later discovered that sometimes it takes a little bit more than thirty days to completely rethink your life. All the same, it was a good start.

Good ways to get started:

- **Reflect:** Think about the five Rs and how you can include them in your daily life.

- **Map out:** Take note of what you throw away and find another solution that is waste free.

- **Analyze:** Go through your bin and find out how much trash you generate in a day.

- **Exclude:** Look at the list of the ten most common types of consumer plastic in the ocean from the previous chapter and remove them for your shopping list.

- **Investigate:** Go visit sustainable shops and stores and find out what alternative products and solutions are out there.

- **Get informed:** Watch documentaries like *A Plastic Ocean, The True Cost, River Blue, Our Planet*, or *Cowspiracy*; they all give you stuff to think about.

- **Engage:** Sign up for sustainable communities, both in real life and online.

- **Find inspiration:** There are so many great videos and guides on the internet—not just my own, but you should still totally share and subscribe!

- **Prepare yourself:** Gather reusable products that fit your routines and have them with you. If you are a coffee drinker, then have a thermos. Are you eating lunch out? Then carry your own cutlery.

A Beginner's Guide

Start by using what you already have. Do you have old Tupperware containers? Then use them until they break. If you have polyester clothing, nail polish, or canned goods, then use them, give them away, sell them, or donate them. At all cost, avoid starting out your sustainable journey by throwing away a bunch of completely functioning stuff, because that is the exact behavior we would like to avoid. When I was a student with a very tight budget, I started my sustainable lifestyle. I would change my plastic products for plastic-free solutions once I had to replace them anyway. The first things I replaced were:

- a plastic dish brush that was changed for a dish brush made of wood or natural fiber bristles;

- a synthetic microfiber cloth that was replaced by a cotton cloth;

- my morning tea in a bag which was replaced by bulk tea in my own container;

- a plastic shopping bag which was changed for an old complimentary canvas tote from a gym I went to back in my hometown. Nothing fancy, just something I had lying in the back of my closet anyway.

Practice saying no to:
- promotional products like balloons and pens
- straws and single-use cutlery from restaurants
- receipts from the supermarket, if given the option
- gifts you do not need
- free samples
- free flyers
- promotional catalogs

You Cannot Buy Your Way Out of the Climate Crisis

If you wish to live a more sustainable life, you will most likely find that some of the things you own will not reflect that wish completely. You will probably also find that you need a lot of new stuff all of the sudden. Social media is not exactly contributing constructively to a realistic depiction of zero waste either; all we see when we search for zero waste online are beautiful, white, clean pantry shelves filled with bulk goods in perfectly identical jars. Often, our first instinct when finding or feeling inspired by a new lifestyle is to go out and purchase a lot of stuff. Specifically stuff that symbolizes this lifestyle change. Take a deep breath and ignore that first thought to buy new stuff, because we cannot buy our way out of the climate crisis.

If we're going to reduce our individual impact, we must consume less. It is that simple—but that does not necessarily make it easy. As the sustainable agenda is becoming more and more widespread, both politically and commercially, more and more products are appearing that claim to be sustainable and green, and we as consumers should not feel bad about buying them. A great example is single-use cutlery. Lots of consumers are realizing that disposable cutlery and plates in plastic are crap, so an increasing number of stores and companies are launching single-use products in bamboo or bioplastic—though still wrapped in plastic.

Some products are green, and some products are more sustainable than others, but it can be difficult to spot them. One reason for this is that it's free for a company to market their products as "biodegradable," "green," "eco-friendly," or "compostable." These buzzwords actually don't require any evidence or certification to use. These products don't have to go through tests or controls to ensure that they live up to their marketing, and therefore, these descriptions are often used in abundance for commercial purposes. When a product is promoted or presented as more sustainable than it actually is, it is called *greenwashing*. This often happens through soft and imprecise descriptions, but it can also be done through visual design. If a product is packaged in mat cardboard or brown/green tones, it automatically inspires certain associations in our brains. These associations usually make us think of rustic, authentic, rural environments. We think of something that is made locally, perhaps by a small, family-owned business. But these associations don't always match the reality of the product's construction or brand. It might very well be that these products are made in a large factory, right next to the products wrapped in shiny and vibrant plastic. Of course, this is not always the case, and there are actually amazing products out there that keep their promises of sustainability, but it can be difficult to navigate which ones are telling the truth.

During the 1980s, most logos and packaging were colorful, often in sharp yellow and red. These colors were eye-catching and got consumers' attention super fast. Think of most fast-food logos: How often are yellow and red primary components of the logo? Today, those colors are not doing it for us anymore. Our attention is often caught by subdued, mild, earthy tones rather than by shiny plastic. Many companies are fully aware of that fact, and they're ready to promote the fantasy of small, rural, family businesses to us.

How Do You Avoid Greenwashing?

Unfortunately, I have been tricked by greenwashing more than once. I have been on cloud nine because of a new plastic-free product in my grocery store, packaged in recycled cardboard and with promises of sustainable production on the front of the rustic box. Full of excitement, I buy the product, only to realize, once I get home, that the cardboard box I have is accompanied by a plastic bag on the inside. Only then did I take a closer look at what the packaging is actually telling me. In microscopic letters, the logo of a large multibillion-dollar corporation was printed on the back; so it was not made by a small sustainable start-up, which was my first impression. The company who made the product were most likely hoping for this exact association, which would explain why their brand and logo was printed in such small letters. On the back of the product, I could also see that recycled paper only accounted for 40 percent of the materials used; the rest was completely new. I also discovered that the ingredients list was far from green as well. I took a quick look in the store and discovered the product didn't contain palm oil or animal products, but printed in tiny letters it said that the product contains FP(K)O. Now that my skepticism had awoken, I decided to find out what that ingredient actually is, and what do you know? It is one of the twenty different names used to describe palm oil in food products— an ingredient which can be found in over 50 percent of processed food products, and which is directly related to deforestation and mass extinction in the rainforest of Borneo, among other places. Yeah, it has become rather difficult to do something right.

Of course, it's impossible to behave perfectly all the time. Sometimes we slip up and buy less-than-ideal products, even though we thought they were sustainable. You will also discover that the products you consider to be the most sustainable can be improved. There is a very delicate balance between making conscious choices and taking all the responsibility for the climate crisis, all in one sitting.

Tips for avoiding greenwashing

- **Find out which company produced the product.** If the company is a commercial giant, then it is very likely that parts of the supply chain don't live up to your sustainable expectations.

- **Find out what the product is made of.** Even though advertisements say that some products are made with recycled materials, you are still allowed to be critical because, often, this only accounts for a small part of the packaging. And as we know, some materials cannot be recycled indefinitely.

- **Read the ingredients list.** A product can contain various types of polluting ingredients, but they're often hidden quite well. Therefore, it can be a good idea to know some of them by heart, so that they are easier to recognize. Make a list and carry that with you in case you forget some terminology.

- **Say no to the biodegradables.** A biodegradable, single-use product is obviously better than plastic disposables, but it's not always necessary to produce single-use biodegradable products. Lots of supermarkets are introducing biodegradable, single-use cutlery, but using regular cutlery from your own kitchen drawer is still more sustainable. "Biodegradable" is often used as a green alibi so a company can keep producing disposables, but unless you compost them yourself, it's very likely that they will not end up biodegrading.

So the company makes a promise that a product will biodegrade, but it is 100 percent the consumers' responsibility to make sure it happens. That is a fairly free-of-charge statement for the company to make then, so there is plenty of space to be critical here.

- **Be skeptical toward composting solutions.** This tip looks a lot like the one above; some greenwashed products will tell you that they are compostable and thus can be perfectly incorporated into a circular, closed system. But compostability can vary a lot, and some products cannot break down in home or backyard composts. One reason is that there is an important difference between a controlled environment, like a test lab, and a home compost: not all materials can break down equally in the various environments. Several studies show that the "biodegradable" plastic that was supposed to be compostable is still completely intact months later, even when exposed to water and soil. These claims can be quite disappointing.

- **Look for certificates.** If you want to find the actual sustainable products in this jungle of greenwashing, you have to look for certificates, recognized third-party labels, and specifications, which can tell you in detail how a product is sustainable without the superficial buzzwords. There are plenty of certificates out there, and it can be difficult to navigate them, as some are easier to obtain than others. However, it's a good idea to know what they represent, as it makes it easier to make an informed decision as a consumer.

These certificates can guide you in the right direction:

- **Green Key:** A green label that is given to restaurants and hotels that live up to the thirteen criteria for sustainable business operation.

- **Green Globe:** A global certificate for sustainable tourism and sustainable tourist attractions.

- **EU Ecolabel:** This can help you identify products which have reduced the impact of their production in regard to extraction of raw materials, processing, utilization, and disposability.

- **Forest Stewardship Council:** An international label that ensures responsible sourcing of forest and lumber products.

- **Cradle to Cradle:** A certificate that is given in five categories and which represents elements like responsible extraction of materials, renewable energy, CO_2 compensation/social responsibility, and recycling abilities.

- **Rainforest Alliance:** Certified companies which responsibly produce coffee, chocolate, tea, fruit, paper, and furniture with a focus on rebuilding and maintaining the environment the materials are extracted from.

- **Global Organic Textile Standard:** A global certificate which ensures the sustainable production of textiles. The standard for the label includes social and sustainable responsibility. The certificate distinguishes between 100 percent organic products and partially organic products.

- **UTZ:** A certificate that is focused on training farmers in responsible and sustainable farming practices.

- **EU Organic Farming:** Certifies that a producer complies with the EU regulations on organic agriculture and trade.

- **Fairtrade:** A certificate that seeks to ensure that employees are being paid a fair wage and are provided with safe working environments.

- **MADE-BY:** A certificate that ensures safe, sustainable, and responsible production of textiles.

Chapter 4

The Plastic You Cannot Avoid

I am going to give you many different pieces of advice in this book; they are going to be applicable in many different situations and some of them won't be equally suitable for all readers. For example, not everyone can avoid plastic altogether. Actually, I would make the argument that no one can avoid plastic altogether, but some people definitely have more opportunities to choose plastic-free alternatives than others. Some people have more spare time to make changes to their lifestyle, and some have more resources with which to realize their green ambitions. Therefore, I think it's only fitting that when we talk about sustainability and what we as consumers can do differently, we also must acknowledge that not everyone has the same opportunities. A lot of people with physical and mental health problems or disabilities are dependent upon plastic products to get through the day. Some people cannot stand up long enough to do dishes and thus have to use disposables if they do not have, or want, other people to help them. Some people cannot hold a mug or bend their neck to drink without a straw. Some people do not have the option to go grocery shopping themselves, and if they want a normal life they have to prioritize a level of convenience that people without disabilities do not need. I think it is everybody's job to acknowledge the difference between necessity and convenience. To some people, plastic products are lifelines, while for others they're meaningless, and because of this, it is extremely important to not only look at the small aspects of the green agenda but also to understand the big picture. The plastic straw has become a symbol of the plastic problem, and because of this, people who rely on straws out of necessity have experienced judgment and harassment, and that is not what sustainability is about—that is not how we save the turtles. Of those eight million metric tons of plastic which end up in our oceans every single year, plastic straws only account for 0.025 percent.

The point is that it's not the necessary use of plastic that has caused the grave issues we see today—it is the misuse of plastic. It is the plastic used in all those situations where it's not actually necessary and where, for many of us, it is completely useless.

So I would like to say something directly to the people who are affected by physical or mental disabilities and who cannot cut plastic out: We can only do the best that we can, and it will look different for each person. Never be ashamed of the trash that is generated from hospital visits, surgeries, medicines, or aids and tools you need to have a normal life. This book is not about shame, and if you, for one reason or another, cannot avoid or refuse a plastic product, then start your sustainable journey someplace else instead of feeling bad about this specific thing. Switch to an energy supplier that uses renewable energy, order plant-based meals, buy secondhand, support local charities or businesses, or whatever else you can think of—it all helps.

Chapter 5

A Zero-Waste Household

A large part of living plastic free is finding ways to minimize plastic around the house, because a lot of the waste the average consumer generates comes from the things we buy for our homes or consume within them. (Of course, some of our impact also comes from external factors, but more on that later.) In my experience, the easiest way to start is by looking inside our homes. We surround ourselves with an intense amount of plastic products every single day, many of which we use for a short while before discarding them. Sometimes it can feel like there are no alternatives or solutions out there, and it's easy to feel overwhelmed by all the things we suddenly feel we're doing wrong. So I want you to remember that it's okay to make the changes one day at a time and just slowly start to reflect and reconsider your routines and habits as you learn new things and run into new challenges.

When I started transitioning to zero waste, I looked around my studio apartment and suddenly saw plastic everywhere, but I chose to treat my new lifestyle as a set of stairs. Every change is a step up, and that made it much less overwhelming. I didn't throw everything I owned away just to buy new things (I also really could not afford that as a student). I also realized that it was not as expensive as I had feared to make green choices. Of course, some things are more expensive, but on the other hand, there was also tons of stuff that I stopped buying, so suddenly I had room to make some other investments. There were also plenty of things I learned how to make myself, and my budget felt that as well. There are countless everyday struggles and homemade solutions which I do not think I have time to go over in this book, but I certainly hope that these guides can prepare you so you can solve whatever other issues you might run into yourself. You can choose to see the recipes in this chapter as starting points, ones which you can keep working on and keep perfecting as much as you want.

Homemade Cleaning Supplies

A rather essential part of zero-waste living is finding one product that can do the job of ten. That way, you do not have to buy ten different products for their own individual purposes. Cleaning products are a good example of how some companies will communicate to you that it's impossible to use what we already have. No, we need a specific cleaner for descaling, we need another to remove fat stains, a third that cleans wooden surfaces, and yet another for tiles. We need one type of cleaner for the kitchen and another for the bathroom. Does that sound familiar? When we look at the amount of cleaning products available, I think most of us have thought, at least once, that all of them cannot possibly be necessary—which they are not. Looking at specialized products from the companies' point of view does make a lot of sense, though. Because selling specialized products to consumers, rather than a universal cleaner, will earn you a lot more money. Beyond that, most cleaning products today are packaged in plastic. As a result of this, I decided to try to make my own cleaning agent.

I was let in on an old recipe for a homemade cleaning agent made with only vinegar and orange peels. Five years ago, I made it for the first time, and it's still the same recipe I use today. Vinegar can often be found in bulk or in glass bottles, but even if you can only find vinegar in plastic packaging, it's still a great alternative to conventional cleaning products—because, again, vinegar is more versatile and can be used for many different things. It is also likely that the plastic used to package the vinegar is easy to recycle because it will probably consist of one type of plastic, whereas many cleaning products are packaged in mixed materials. This is how I see it: vinegar can replace over ten other products at home, so if nothing else, it's one plastic bottle instead of ten.

Ingredients:

- ¼ gallon of vinegar
- the peels of two oranges
- a wide-set bottle

Pour the vinegar into the bottle or container; make sure it's wide set so the orange peels can go in as well. When adding the peels, make sure that they are completely covered by the vinegar. Let it sit for seven days, until it's ready for use.

This vinegar-orange blend had several advantages. It absorbs bad odors, so it can be used to get rid of smells on surfaces simply by wiping a cloth covered in the solution over the surface and then letting it air dry. You can also put a small jar of the solution into the fridge if you are battling unpleasant smells. For general cleaning, you can also mix the vinegar solution with warm water (somewhere between a quarter and a half gallon for a half cup of vinegar) and use it all around the house. The orange contributes antibacterial qualities and the acidic juice in the peel is great for cleaning limescale stains or kitchen grease.

Other cleaning tips:

- Use a broom or other nonelectric appliances and tools to clean smaller messes.
- Choose a vacuum without a bag to avoid the waste when throwing them away.
- Avoid microfiber cloths and other synthetic materials.
- Open windows and dust off surfaces rather than using cleaning agents daily.

Munkholm

Rosmarin & Cit...

Dish wash

Dish soap

Unless you have access to a bulk store or a health store, it can be pretty difficult to find dish soap without plastic, but it's not impossible. I have found dish soaps in glass containers from an online eco shop, which simply shows that sometimes we have to make use of the internet to make our plastic-free dreams come true. You can also find solid dish soap, which you simply wet with your dish brush before using. This soap comes with minimal packaging.

Brushes and cloths

One of the first things I replaced in my home was my dish brush. It was an easy switch because more and more supermarkets had started to sell plastic-free dish brushes made from wood and bamboo. The brushes that I think are the absolute best are the ones which have organic and natural plant-based bristles. They can easily be upcycled or taken apart for composting. To "upcycle" means to find a new function for a product that would otherwise have been thrown away. In this case, it meant using the brush handle as supports for my plants. You can also use them in your garden by writing the names of herbs or directions on them. If you buy a wooden dish brush, you have to be sure to not leave it in wet spots, as the wood reacts poorly to long-term moisture and will start to rot. So find a dry spot to keep it, rather than chucking it in the sink. I have mine in a jar next to my sink, where I can leave it to dry.

Easy swaps for the kitchen:

- Use a dish brush made from wood and natural fiber rather than plastic.
- Use a sponge made of coconut fiber or other plants.
- Try cloths made of cotton; they are easy to DIY as well.

Conventional cleaning or dish cloths are often made from plastic and cannot be recycled after use. Furthermore, they release microplastic every time you use them. Alternatively, you can make cloths from materials that can be composted. If you do not have a compost, you can put the cloths with organic waste, but you can also use them to sprout seeds of chives or cress—which is pretty badass. Many cleaning sponges are made from a synthetic foam material, but they can also be made from plant fibers. To avoid your natural cloths and sponges tearing up or falling apart too fast, it's important also to store them away from moisture and let them dry completely after each use. I have a little arrangement in my kitchen window where I let them dry in the sun.

Alternatives to Foil and Film

You know the scene: You are about to wrap the leftovers from your dinner, so you reach down to your kitchen drawers and get your cling film. With some difficulty, because it keeps getting stuck to its damn self all the time, you rip off a piece and wrap it around your bowl. The next day, when you're warming up your food, you will toss that film in your bin. The sheer amount of cling film and aluminum foil the average household consumes is larger than we think because those products are both cheap and convenient. They also just suck when measured on the green-o-meter because cling film cannot be recycled, so it often ends in a landfill—and sadly, the fate of most aluminum foil is pretty much the same. However, the foil can actually be recycled if we take the extra time to rinse it off before sorting it. Luckily, there are some equally easy and convenient alternatives to these everyday products. If you want, you can mix and match and find out which solution works the best for you. I know I use a combination of these options every week:

A plate: The easiest solution is probably to place a plate on top of another plate and store the food in between. It is reliable, free, and simply zero waste.

Wax wraps: If the leftovers are leaving the house, two plates quickly become a hassle. Instead, I add wax wraps to the mix. The wax wrap is made from a piece of fabric with a wax coating on each side (preferably plant-based wax). These wraps can be washed and reused over and over again. You fold the food into the fabric, warm it up in your hands so the wax adapts to the shape, and voila, the food is concealed in the wrap.

Containers: But what if you have some leftovers that are not solid foods, like soup? Here you will not get far with either plates or wax wrap. A solid container is the perfect solution. A mason jar, or an old upcycled peanut butter jar, can be used both in the fridge and on the go. Simply wash them with your dishes after use.

Toilet paper

You can also find several sustainable alternatives to toilet paper, as well as green versions of the option we are already familiar with. We often regard toilet paper as a product that is used all over the world— but that is not actually the case. A good sustainable investment, which will also show positive financial effects, is a bidet or a bidet attachment. By flushing instead of wiping after each visit to the toilet, there are a whole lot of resources that can be saved. Bidets are widely used in many places around the world. They come both as a full installment next to the toilet itself or as handy attachments that are installed onto your toilet that take up no extra space. Another alternative is reusable fabric cloth instead of toilet paper. It is a solution I have not tried myself, but I thought I would mention it anyway. I do, however, know many people who have combined the bidet solution with reusable rolls made from cut-up cotton fabric that had once been shirts. Now you are probably thinking: "Damn that is disgusting, I would never ever in a million years do that." I understand that thought, because once we have normalized one restroom routine, all other options seem bizarre, but studies have actually found that using a bidet is more hygienic than simply wiping away.

Another solution, which perhaps looks and feels a little bit homier, is toilet paper made from recycled paper that is unbleached and wrapped in plastic-free materials. You can often find these options for wholesale at stores that professional cleaning stores use, i.e., a store that mainly has other businesses as customers. Or you can look at online options. Before I learned that many green webshops also sell sustainable toilet paper, I used to buy mine wholesale because that kind is usually not wrapped in plastic but rather in paper or cardboard, in comparison to the options we know from our local supermarkets.

Recipe for Toilet Tabs

One of the worst types of household chemicals is toilet cleaner, but it is possible to make a healthier and more sustainable alternative at home. You can make your own toilet tabs, which require only a few ingredients and minimal packaging.

Ingredients:

- 1¼ cup of baking soda
- ½ cup of citric acid
- ¼ cup of dish soap
- 5–6 drops of essential oils
- an ice cube tray or a small baking mold

Mix the four ingredients in a bowl and pour the mix into a mold of choice—I prefer an ice cube tray. Place the tray in the freezer for at least one hour. These tabs can stay fresh for months and you only have to use one tab per cleaning. Use either a spoon or a spatula to pop your tabs out of the mold and into a glass jar or other storage container.

Easy bathroom swaps:

- toothbrushes made from wood or bamboo
- toothpaste tabs like Denttabs
- biodegradable dental floss
- reusable cotton rounds
- solid hand soap
- shampoo and conditioner bars
- safety razors

Laundry

Detergent: We use an unbelievable amount of products to clean our clothes—yeah, laundry can also come with its own jungle of specialized products. And just like with other cleaning products, most of them can be replaced by one. Lots of detergents already come in cardboard packaging, so that is a quick swap right there: choosing a powder detergent rather than liquid detergents.

Soap nuts: But there are also other types of alternatives to the well-known detergent powders. Lots of detergents come with a downside because many of the active enzymes of the detergent compound are designed to dissolve organic tissue. That may sound great, because organic tissue forms the dirt and stains on our clothes such as grass stains or curry soup, but these effects can also come with some health concerns. Skin is also organic tissue. A natural alternative is soap nuts. These dried nuts can be bought in health stores and via online webshops. They contain a large amount of saponin, which is activated when it comes into contact with water and works as a natural soap. You put four to six

nuts in a bag and throw it in with your laundry, and that is it. The nuts can last for up to four washes and can be composted afterward. Do be aware, though, that with the rising popularity of soap nuts, some companies and distributors are taking advantage of the communities that naturally produce them in India. Not all soap nuts are produced ethically and sustainably, and some are also wrapped in plastic, so look out for companies that build up the communities they work with.

Fabric softeners: I know a lot of people who are allergic to fabric softeners. The reason why is because they contain large amounts of synthetic perfumes. These clog your pores, and they have a devastating effect on water systems and biodiversity. The solution is simply to avoid them. Fabric softener does not have any necessary function that you cannot achieve using other, less harmful, products. But they're still sold all around the world because they give us an idea of cleanliness due to their being loaded with perfumes—and, as we all know, something isn't clean until it smells like a lamb running in a blooming

field. If you like your laundry to come with some scent, you can use a few drops of essential oils instead—I personally really like lemon and rosemary.

Drying: An easy hack which can reduce the impact of your laundry load by half is skipping the electric dryer. They are intensely energy consuming, but they also reduce the lifetime of your clothes because drying them in a machine is rough on the materials. Instead, dry your clothes outside if the weather calls for it—or in a room with proper ventilation.

Laundry and microplastic: As mentioned before, synthetic clothes, like those made with polyester, release microplastic every time you wash them. The solution is *not* to throw away all your synthetic clothes but instead to wash them as gently as possible. Moreover, you can also get filtration bags that catch the microfibers before they go into the water system. It is definitely better than doing nothing, and the fibers can be tossed in the bin rather than getting scattered in the water.

Compost Guide

Why is composting always such an important part of the zero-waste household? I see more and more cities implementing organic waste recycling, but it is important to remember that this isn't exactly the same as composting. You can read more about organic waste recycling and bio-gas in Chapter 2. Composting is a completely circular system wherein organic matter is transformed into mold. Composting can be a really good move because mold is great for home plants and can be used as a garden fertilizer.

Community compost: You can ask around in your neighborhood for community composting facilities or options. If there are some, you can make room in your freezer for your compostable waste and make a weekly trip to the compost to toss it.

Home compost, outside:
Perhaps you have a yard, and in that case, you can easily make your own compost outside. Organic matter can easily break down in soil with help from bacteria and small animals—as well as wind and weather.

Home compost, inside: There is also a solution for people without a yard or any outside space; you can have a compost inside. When done right, it does not smell at all and poses no health risks.

Worm compost

Having a compost comes with many advantages, even if you live in a small flat. One of the easiest ways of composting, and the one that requires the smallest amount of work, is a worm compost. It does not smell at all, and it is a habit that is easily integrated into a normal daily routine, even if you are on a busy schedule. Find a container that seals shut—you can buy specialized composting containers, but a plastic container with a lid also works fine. Here, I actually encourage the use of plastic, but it can be used over and over again, and that is always something.

What you need to remember about composts is that they need oxygen to survive. So it is important to ventilate the mold or drill holes in the lid so there is a constant flow of fresh air. You can also find composting containers made from plant-based plastic or bamboo fibers that can do the trick. Fill your container with a good amount of soil, add your worms (which can be bought online, or you can go digging). They reproduce rather fast and go through a surprising amount of organic material if they're healthy. This way, you can easily dispose of your organic waste without it winding up in a landfill. Most composting containers can be placed both inside and outside, just be aware of degrees below freezing.

What is compostable?

- **Clothes**. Yeah, clothes. Organic materials like wool and cotton are actually compostable. Synthetic clothes are not compostable (figure that), and materials with plastic coatings are not compostable either. But a normal cotton shirt can be broken down in your own circular system in your compost.

- **Plant-based kitchen waste**. All your scraps from salads, soups, stews, and sandwiches can be composted. Some scraps might take longer to break down than others, like banana peels. Other types of kitchen waste are broken down super fast, like coffee grounds or tea leaves.

- **Paper**. Untreated or uncoated paper and cardboard is also easily composted—and in only a few weeks. As long as the paper is not shiny or treated with a coating, you can, with good conscience, feed it to your worms.

What is not compostable?

- **Animal products**. Even though animal products can be broken down in industrial composts and organic recycling, they should be avoided in home composts. The smell of meat, bones, fat, and skin can easily attract a huge fan base of mice, rats, and cats. Your odor-free compost will not be so odor free anymore either.

- **Citrus fruits and onions**. Yes, it seems rather illogical, but if you have a worm compost, you should avoid citruses and onions. They are both too acidic and can kill your worms, a.k.a. destroying the compost. If you have a garden compost, or just one without worms, you do not have to worry about this. The citrus peels can also easily be used to make a zero-waste cleaning agent, and the onion scraps are great if you're making broth.

- **Coffee filters and teabags**. Even though the contents of the bags and filters are easily composted, the same cannot be said for the containers. Many filters and tea bags are made from mixed materials and sometimes they contain plastic, and you do not want plastic in your compost.

- **Stool.** You know, not from people, or...actually, you know what, also from people. But I am specifically referring to stool from animals, like pets—and especially carnivorous pets. Their poop can contain micro-organisms and parasites that are rather dangerous, both to your compost and to you if you use the compost as potting soil or fertilizer. Stool from herbivorous animals like horses and cows is okay in composts though, as long as they're not given feed that contain animal products.

Chapter 6

ELECTRONICS

Let's talk a little about electronics. Electronic devices take up a lot of room in our everyday lives; the average consumer utilizes everything from televisions and cell phones to refrigerators and microwave ovens every single day. However, those electronic devices do not come without an impact—it can require up to five hundred pounds of raw materials to produce a single smartphone. Electronics like smartphones are made of several raw materials, but one of the most essential is aluminum. Now, aluminum is not necessarily the biggest climate villain of all time. In the recycling guide, we established that aluminum can be used in a closed recycling system without degrading in quality, and—fun fact—at this point in time, we have extracted and produced enough aluminum that we technically never have to mine for more raw material again; we can simply recycle what we already have, over and over. Sadly, most electronic devices are still made with new aluminum because it can be purchased cheaply. The reason it is cheap is because many of the components used in aluminum production are extracted from the earth by hand in developing countries, and mine workers are paid incredibly unfair and small wages for their dangerous labor. But what happens to our electronic devices once they break or become outdated?

E-Waste and Disposal

Discarded electronic devices are categorized as e-waste, or electronic waste, and Denmark is one of the countries in the world that produces the most e-waste per person. Actually, an average Dane generates fifty-three pounds of e-waste every year, and that is more than the average of the US, Sweden, the UK, and Germany, all of which also have rather high waste averages in comparison to the global average. E-waste represents 2 percent of America's trash in landfills, but it equals 70 percent of overall toxic waste, and according to the EPA, e-waste is still the fastest growing municipal waste stream in America on average.

We produce all this e-waste partly because we like having the newest editions of things. Consumers want the latest updates, the trendiest model, and as a result, we buy new smartphones, tablets, laptops, and more whenever a new version is launched. The average consumer owns a smartphone for eighteen months before replacing it and throwing the old one away. Furthermore, only a very small percentage of electronic devices are recycled—11 percent is the global average. It is both very energy intense and polluting to recycle e-waste, and the most important components of any device are the metals it is made of. Because of this, the devices are melted down to extract those metals again.

I do not know if you can imagine what happens if you try to light a smartphone on fire? It isn't data I would recommend you try to collect yourself, because burning electronics releases lots of toxic fumes. It isn't ideal for air quality or the people nearby. Many types of e-waste contain dangerous and toxic components like lead, mercury, zinc, chrome, nickel, and flame retardants. When these components are exposed to high temperatures, they can cause a lot of damage; especially when we consider that a lot of e-waste is exported to developing countries without the proper facilities to ensure a safe recycling or disposal process, both for the environment and the workers. Many tech companies often send their outdated devices to landfills in countries without strict waste management and regulation. It is a rather common practice for companies to exploit workers in areas affected by poverty when disposing of their waste. When e-waste is exposed to heat, it will release harmful chemicals into the air and the atmosphere, and with fifty million metric tons of e-waste generated globally every year, the effect of this practice is not insignificant. A lot of e-waste also ends up in open landfills where the chemical components in the devices will slowly cause soil and groundwater pollution, which negatively affects both flora and fauna. The huge problem with e-waste is the fact that we generate so much of it, but luckily there are steps we can take as consumers to prevent a lot of the waste.

Pre-Loved Gadgets

First of all, use your electronic devices as long as you can—as long as they are still functional. You can ask yourself if it is strictly necessary to acquire the brand-new model and the latest gadgets. (Psst! It rarely is.) Companies that sell electronics spend incredible amounts of resources on making their products stand out as prestigious, and replace old devices with new ones as a luxurious act, even if the difference is minimal. For the companies, this is a financially clever move, and it is up to the consumer to think twice and not become intrigued by their new hardware and sophisticated design. But what if the phone you already have is actually broken and cannot be repaired? In that case, you don't have to buy the brand-new model either. Instead, look at the secondhand, pre-loved options because they are plentiful. Because of today's toss-and-buy-new culture, it is easy to buy electronics that are both modern and well-functioning.

There are also several companies that specialize in secondhand smartphones, often with the same service and with additional guarantees—the same goes for laptops. But, as with all other secondhand purchases, it requires research and patience. Before going down to the store to purchase a brand-new phone, it never hurts to look at Facebook Marketplace or the secondhand sites.

> ## Where to buy secondhand electronics
>
> - **Smartphones and laptops:** Use the internet to find a company in your country that specializes in secondhand devices.
> - **Televisions, headphones, and smaller gadgets:** Use secondhand platforms like Facebook Marketplace, Craigslist, or any equivalent.
> - **Fridges, washing machines, etc.:** Search online, or buy secondhand from other people.

Planned Obsolescence and Repairs

There is something else we should talk about, and sadly, it is one of those things that are not up to the individual consumer to change, at least for now. Planned obsolescence is something that affects most electronic devices today. It means that when an electronic device is produced, an expiration date is built into the design of the device—a point in time at which it will simply stop functioning, when new software will no longer be compatible with the device, or when it simply cannot be fixed. This will force the consumer to upgrade to a newer device. Perhaps you're thinking: "Is that not just a sign of my phone getting older? There is nothing sketchy about that, is that not just how it is?" Yes, that is just how it is, but planned obsolescence is actually an essential part of the foundation of new electronic devices. It has been proven over and over again that it is completely possible to create and design software and hardware which does not act this way—however, the profit margin is obviously lower. Perhaps you recognize this from your own smartphone: a brand drops a new model, and not many weeks after, your own phone starts demanding updates. When the updates are complete, your phone starts running slower and you sense a decrease in software quality. In reality, this is the company nudging you in the direction of their newest model. In 2017, several big tech companies confessed that they let updates damage older phones to force consumers to buy new ones. Because of this, we cannot hold on to our old smartphones forever—the manufacturer made sure of that. This is also the reason why electronics cannot successfully become a part of circular economies, because they're built to be discarded and designed to end up as trash. If you have issues with your smartphone or laptop, it can actually be quite detrimental to have it looked at by the official store that distributes them. There are countless examples of companies' repair teams declaring a product unfixable or "out of date" when an independent repair shop is able to fix it in a matter of minutes. Therefore, it is a great idea to seek assistance at small independent shops that specialize in phone or computer repairs.

Where does e-waste come from?

- Sixty percent of e-waste comes from household appliances.
- Seven percent comes from smartphone, computers, and printers.

Another problem that consumers can face is that the price for repairs can exceed the price of a new product. Moreover, many companies are making sure that consumers cannot fix their devices themselves by making it impossible—or just really expensive—to buy individual parts. It is a problem that is hard to get around as a consumer, especially if you're dealing with a broken freezer and an ice cream cake that is dripping down onto the floor. If you can afford it, getting your devices and appliances fixed rather than buying new is more sustainable. If you have to replace them and it is impossible to find any secondhand options, the most sustainable choice is choosing to buy from a company with a well-established repair policy/system or a company which does something extra to ensure sustainable production. The best option, the most sustainable option, might very well not be the cheapest option in many cases, so avoiding the cheapest products might be a good idea.

Extend a product's lifetime by:

- repairing, buying secondhand, and postponing renewal;
- handing in electronics for recycling.

In 2019, while I was still in the process of writing the Danish version of this book, I was on the train on my way to give a lecture. I was sitting across from two women, one of them in her sixties I would guess, the other in her early twenties. It did not seem like they knew each other, but they were making polite conversation. The older woman took her cell phone from her handbag to read a text message she got from her granddaughter (I only know this because she read it out loud). When she had read the text, the younger woman broke out in laughter. I looked up from my laptop to see what was going on and what was apparently so funny. The older woman was the owner of a smartphone that (going by a quick eyeballing guestimate) was more than three years old, and the sight of the phone made the younger women react with: "That is a really old phone you have there! Sorry, I did not mean to laugh." The older woman was not at all bothered by the reaction, she shrugged her shoulders and said that it was her granddaughter's old phone and that it was able to perform all the tasks she needed it for. I think this is a great example of how we usually talk about electronics. This displays the mindset of many consumers, and how we often crave the newer models even if they're quite unessential for us. But there is also some prestige in this mindset, or for lack of better words, some bragging/flexing effect. However, if we all treated electronics and renewals a little bit like old ladies, we would automatically have a more sustainable relationship with our devices.

Data Storage and Streaming

In the context of electronics, it is also relevant to mention data storage and streaming because these everyday tools have a bigger impact on our climate than we might expect. We save countless files in "the cloud," which includes images, music, videos, e-mails, and important documents—but where is the cloud? When we upload something to the internet, it requires energy, and even though it seems like the internet is this abstract and ethereal thing, it is actually a very physical place in the world. Access to the internet and data storage does not happen on its own. It requires huge data centers which run on electricity. A data center is what keeps you online, and it is estimated that there were more than 500,000 data centers in the world as of 2019. Combined, they use as much power as the entirety of Great Britain. The average consumer may utilize data storage, but most companies are using the service as well, and there is a big difference in how they store documents. Some data centers are run on renewable energy; however, most are still operating on fossil fuels. Globally, we store so much information, a.k.a. files, that the impact of data storage in terms of emissions is almost equivalent to that of airplanes (air travel accounts for 2.5 percent of global emissions and it is estimated that data storage and streaming account for about 2 percent). Moreover, it is estimated that the emissions released from data centers can double every fourth year.

Storing data does not account for the biggest part of consumers' private internet consumption—streaming music and movies, as well as online gaming, is where we leave the biggest online impact. Every time you stream your favorite song or binge a show online, you consume energy. Actually, these activities require so much energy that a study from the University of Oslo showed that the packaging you avoid by streaming rather than buying physical copies of content is almost neutralized by the impact of the energy consumption. This is the case if we only look at CO_2 emissions. The quantity of plastic related to movies and music has decreased from sixty-one million metric tons to eight million metric tons between 2000 and 2016 in the US. However, this drop is neutralized by the increased energy consumption of our larger online presence. So is it actually better to go back to CDs and DVDs? No, not really. However, in order to consume these online services in a sustainable way, we need data centers to switch from fossil fuels to green energy sources. Moreover, there are other small things we as consumers can do to have greener online habits.

Greener habits online

Avoid using streaming as background noise when you are sleeping or doing other chores or activities.

- If you already have a physical copy, then use that rather than streaming it online.

- If you want to binge a show, then watch it with friends and family on the same device, rather than watching it individually on multiple devices.

- If you own an external hard drive, then use that to store files rather than leaving everything online.

- Think about what you store, and clean up your online drives to avoid storing unnecessary files.

In 2017, Greenpeace produced a report called *Clicking Clean—Who is Winning the Race to Build a Green Internet*, which accounted for the impact of different online streaming platforms. The report gives an overview of the different companies and which green initiatives they support and operate with. Based on that information, the companies are assigned scores that can help you make an informed decision regarding which platforms to support. The report can be downloaded via ClickClean.org/international/en/

Chapter 7

CLOTHING

I have always loved clothes. It is a form of self-expression; it is a way of letting people know who you are. When I was ten years old, my mom stopped dressing me for school. She used to lay out the outfit I was supposed to wear that day on my bed, but I was the world's most stubborn child and knew exactly what I wanted to wear: a red satin clip-on tie from a costume shop, knee high socks with stripes and the tip cut off so they could be used as fingerless gloves, and a basketball jersey with thick red sewing thread sewn in and out of the large holes on the front of the shirt. (Yes, I made it myself, and I was super proud.) Later, I started experimenting with darker aesthetics, and on the day I entered seventh grade I had a pitch-black (self-cut), shoulder-length hairdo, black nail polish, canvas shoes with skull prints, and a desert-dry, black eyeliner thoroughly outlining my upper and under lash line. This image still makes my parents shake their heads, I am certain. By the end of high school, I had found a job as a street-style photographer and fashion commentator for Copenhagen Fashion Week, so I spent a large amount of my time running across the cobbled streets in front of the Copenhagen Court House in tiny stilettos while trying to snatch the perfect picture of some off-duty models. In the beginning of my zero-waste journey, I used my style to express my lifestyle change. I went through a hippie phase, as well as a more minimalistic phase. However, today, I have recovered my life of style and fashion, loud prints, and statement pieces. Sustainability is not an aesthetic, or a certain style, it is a method. I still have fun, and I love expressing myself and experimenting with different styles and looks. The point is, we need to feel good about what we wear.

However, the fact is we buy too much, and the clothes from the fast-fashion industry have a huge impact on the planet.

In this chapter we are going to talk about the impact of fast fashion. The perspective of this chapter is based on the fact that many consumers are buying way more than they need. As such, the commentary will be directed toward overconsumption. I am absolutely aware that not everybody is buying cheap clothes for leisure, because it is fun, or because that way they can buy so much more than they need to. Some people don't have the option not to shop for these brands because of budget or accessibility issues. It is important for me to highlight that the critique directed toward the fast-fashion industry is not a critique of those consumers who don't have the choice, or privilege, to refuse it.

What Is Fast Fashion?

Most of the clothes that are being bought today are produced as so-called fast fashion. It is an expression the clothing industry originally introduced to describe the fast pace with which clothes are designed, promoted, and sold to consumers. The term also covers the speed with which most clothes today are produced and thrown away. If you think about fashion chains and clothing stores, chances are they're fast fashion, because around 95 percent of all clothes produced today are produced with fast-fashion practices and that is a huge problem. The fast-fashion industry is the fifth-most-polluting industry in the world, a place it has earned because of water pollution, emission of greenhouse gases, production waste, poor waste management, and through the impact of the production of materials (including cotton production). The fashion industry is responsible for more than 1,875 million metric tons of CO_2 emissions every year and utilizes over 2.1 billion gallons of water. On top of that, there are transportation emissions involved in the transfer from the countries where the garments are produced to the shelves in department stores. A defining factor of fast fashion is the price, and the price is undeniably linked to how the clothes are produced—namely, in sweatshops. Fast-fashion companies are saving a ton of money by outsourcing their production of clothing to countries where factory workers have no rights and where people are living in poverty. "Sweatshop" is the term used to describe a factory or a workshop that keeps people working in inhumane conditions, usually by requiring intensely long hours of work in dangerous conditions and for very low wages. Saving money on production is something that affects the entire fast-fashion industry and, as a result, several studies have found proof of falsified documents and construction agreements. The documentary *River Blue* uncovers how the practices of fast-fashion companies are linked to dangerous working environments, water pollution, and little-to-no regard for managing dangerous chemicals and waste products. The collapse of the building known as the Rana Plaza in Bangladesh in 2013 cost 1,134 factory workers their lives and wounded an additional 2,500 people. Why? Because when we want to produce a lot of stuff quickly and cheaply, other areas of production are disregarded.

Facts about sweatshop workers:

- In Bangladesh, the average monthly pay of a garment worker is $33, while the living costs are twice as high.
- It is illegal for factory workers to discuss wages or form unions.
- The number of sexual assaults on women in sweatshops is constantly increasing.

- Sweatshop workers can have twelve-to-sixteen-hour shifts.
- Forced child labor is not an uncommon practice.

Sweatshops have existed for decades, and they have never been a secret. If you ask people who they think their clothes are made by, most people know that they're not super-duper ethically produced. Okay, so a global billion-dollar industry treats their employees badly. That can seem like a pretty big issue. How can you change that by yourself? The fact is that the fashion industry has evolved into what it is today because people buy their products. They produce what they know they can sell. The first step is to stop giving them your money. Several brands have sent the four seasons into retirement (you know, summer, autumn, spring, and winter) in favor of fifty-two new seasons. This way, they get to launch new styles every week and thus nudge consumers to continuously buy new clothes. As a result of this change, clothes are being produced dangerously fast and this has consequences not just for factory workers but also for our planet.

The fashion industry produces so many clothes that no one could possibly buy them all, and because of this, millions of tons of new, unworn clothes end up being thrown away every year. A majority of the discarded clothes end up in open landfills where they cannot biodegrade, and there they will emit methane for decades to come. But we do need some clothes, and is it not better that people in Bangladesh, India, and China have small wages rather than no wages at all? It is true that we do need clothes, but the extreme production of the industry and the way we consume clothes today are not born out of necessity and basic living needs; they are a result of luxury, convenience, and overconsumption. One single cotton

T-shirt requires more than 710 gallons of water to produce; however, many consumers buy dozens and throw them away just as quickly without thinking about the intense amount of resources the garment represents. If consumers in the West only bought and consumed what they needed, the industry would look entirely different. And yes, it is a good idea to create jobs in poor areas and developing countries—that sounds pretty noble. But the way the industry is mistreating and exploiting their workers today has nothing to do with nobility or charity. Both consumers and brands have a responsibility here because it costs money to pay workers fair wages, it costs money to improve and secure work environments so they're no longer dangerous, and it costs money to avoid water pollution. This is money many consumers will have a hard time paying because we have grown accustomed to low prices. The cheaper, the better, and what we don't pay has a huge price on the other end of the supply chain.

But it isn't fair to leave all the responsibility with the consumer. Another part of the problem with fast fashion is the intensely high markup on the products that the industry is producing. The markup refers to the difference between what it costs to produce an item and the price the consumer pays. Most stores don't pay an awful lot to have their products made, so if a cotton T-shirt costs thirty dollars in the store, it might very well have cost the brand less than half a dollar to make it. Where does the rest of the money go if they don't pay workers or improve the supply chain? The majority of the money we pay for a product goes to the CEOs and to pay for branding and marketing. The people at the top of the fashion industry are among the world's richest businesspeople. However, even with billions in their bank accounts, they continuously ignore needs like basic safety, fair wages, and any regard for the environment.

How to create green fashion habits:

- Watch documentaries about fast fashion, like *River Blue* and *The True Cost*.

- Avoid using shopping as a leisure activity and limit purchases to the necessities.

- Avoid trends, and buy only what you know you will love for a long time instead.

- If you can, think about other advantages of products rather than just their cheap price tag; cheaper is not better.

But what does all of this stuff about production and ethics have to do with zero waste anyway? As we will continuously discover throughout this book, waste is about much more than what we throw into our own bins. There are billions of tons of waste and trash related to the big global industries, so if we want to better ourselves and become informed consumers, it is really important to be aware of these underlying systems of pollution and exploitation, because it is all connected. Several years ago, a friend of mine sent a picture from her shopping trip and beneath the picture it read: "Look, zero-waste shopping!" The picture showed two new dresses from a fast-fashion brand. She had refused a plastic bag, so the only visible trash was from the small price tags attached to the dresses. And it's true, it is a rather small amount of trash that has reached her hands, but actually a ton of trash is hidden behind the scenes. When new clothes are packaged from the sweatshop and sent to the stores, each individual garment is packaged in its own plastic bag. Additionally, there is transportation waste as well as emissions. Textiles from the fashion industry are also treated with harsh and dangerous chemicals to achieve a certain distressed look or style. Leather and denim, for instance, are especially problematic when it comes to chemical waste because they are often treated many times before shipment. Conventional cotton production (nonorganic cotton) is one of the biggest consumers of pesticides and insecticides in the world, and textile colorants are the second largest polluter of fresh water, the number one polluter being agriculture. So if you want to live with zero waste, it is essential to stop and reflect upon the overall impact of the industries and companies we support. Here is a step away from fast fashion, a step closer to zero waste.

How to Spot the Sustainable Brands

Sustainable and ethical products cost more than products made in sweatshops, mainly because you pay for conscientious practices everywhere in the supply chain. As a result, most of us will not be able to buy the same amount of sustainable clothes as we did fast fashion. It also means that one cannot necessarily treat the act of acquiring new clothes as the same leisure activity that shopping might have been previously, but luckily, there are plenty of other things to do. While sustainably and ethically produced clothing is often more expensive than fast fashion, it is seldom because some CEO is reaping the profits. Rather, it is because the people who made the clothes can make a living off their salary—instead of being paid three cents per hour. Another reason why sustainable clothes can be more expensive is because sustainable production methods, materials, and techniques are often more costly due to supply and demand. When trying to figure out if a company is sustainable, it can be a good idea to look for these signs:

1. Do they have actual certificates to back up their claims?

As previously mentioned, it does not cost anything to brand a product as *sustainable*, *green*, *eco-friendly*, or *natural*, and the company does not have to disclose any information about their production to use these buzzwords. Of course, that does not mean that misleading consumers is okay (because it is not!). So look for third-party regulations and certifications that can document how true their claims are: look to Fairtrade, GOTS, and Who Made Your Clothes, among others, for guidelines.

2. Is the supply chain transparent?

Does the company seem honest and transparent? Again, it is a question of documentation and of how the brand communicates their efforts to the consumer. Companies that treat their employees well are often not scared of showing it, and will frequently go the extra mile to show what goes on behind the scenes. It isn't a good sign if you cannot find any information about the production of a company's clothes. Similarly, brands that don't utilize harmful chemicals, pesticides, and dyes will be sure to communicate that to you with receipts, as the opposite is generally the norm. The more open the company is, the better.

3. Is there consistency between the price and the product?

Textiles are expensive to produce if produced sustainably, as it takes both time and effort to produce good quality. Thus, a pair of denim jeans cannot both be produced sustainably and cost twenty dollars. On the other hand, a product can also be extremely expensive and still not support a sustainable or ethical supply chain. It can be an advantage to refuse the idea that designer labels are better, because they are not necessarily better for the planet or for the people who produce them. It can be a good idea to look for quality and transparency, rather than both cheap convenience and prestigious labels.

4. Can you get in touch with the brand?

If you have any questions as a consumer, the best course of action is reaching out to the company themselves. However, sometimes it can be difficult to get a concrete answer, or get a hold of them at all, especially when working with bigger brands. Maybe that is because most large brands are not super interested in answering a ton of specific, production-related questions or generally dwelling too much on what goes on behind the billboard advertisements. If you try to contact a fast-fashion brand, you will most likely receive an automated, or at least rehearsed, answer, and that is typically not a sign of transparency. Once again, sustainable brands will be much more likely to reply with a detailed and to-the-point answer because they have nothing to hide. If you feel like the company is avoiding your questions, or refusing to reply in a straightforward way, it can often be interpreted as lack of transparency.

Kicking the Habit of Fast Fashion

I remember having a really tough time giving up fast fashion—especially those cheap sales. When I was in high school, I was browsing through the discount racks at fast-fashion shops, spending all my money on this clothing that I did not even need. But while gradually growing into and learning about the zero-waste lifestyle, the urge to go shopping for fun slowly faded away. As you practice saying no and refusing what you don't need, these things will automatically become easier. The easy and convenient part of shopping is also something I think we should address. Because why is it that convenient? Most online stores have free return policies, and both physical and online stores are constantly advertising big sales; both of these actions heavily impact consumers' shopping habits. The easier and quicker it is to shop, the more likely it is that we will end up buying things we do not need. Shops rarely want to extend the shopping time of shoppers, because the longer we have to reflect upon our purchases, the more likely it is we will regret them. Have you ever noticed what kind of music most stores, especially clothing stores, are playing? It is very fast paced and upbeat, and those tunes also nudge us into making quicker decisions. If you are considering buying something nonessential, then wait a while—my personal advice is to wait a week before making up your mind.

> **Things to think about:**
>
> - You do not have to buy new clothes for every party or event.
> - You can easily style what you already have in new interpretative ways.

The price is often the reason why many consumers choose fast fashion over sustainable brands—for instance, because we expect to get as much for our money as possible. However, another reason could be that some consumers might not be able to afford to pay more than what fast fashion is charging. Luckily, there is a solution to such an issue. When I started my zero-waste journey, I was often startled by the price of sustainable goods; I never thought I would be able to afford them. But, over time, I realized something: If you start practicing a sustainable lifestyle and begin consuming less, the way you spend money changes drastically—because suddenly you're refraining from buying various products. Living sustainably can save you money because it often comes with the refusal of, for example, impulse purchases, unnecessary upgrades, expensive steaks, and much more. However, if you only change one thing, and then continue the rest of your life as before, you will not experience that same shift in your budget—then the sustainable swap will become an extra expense. Thus, we not only have to buy less, but also greener and better.

Secondhand and Clothing Swaps

Supporting sustainable brands is a really good idea, because the more support they get, the more common sustainable shopping habits become. But it can also be slightly utopian to expect everyone to only buy from sustainable brands. Luckily, there is also the secondhand option. When you buy clothes in thrift shops, you're not supporting fast fashion, because the profits go toward charity and maintenance of the store instead. At this point in time, enough clothes have been produced that we technically do not need to produce anything new again, at least for a very long time. Because of this, buying secondhand is an ideal way of making your wardrobe more sustainable. Clothing swaps and secondhand apps are also great ways of avoiding buying brand-new things.

Gittemarie's guide to thrift shops

When thrift shopping, it is a great idea to be open-minded. Looking for one very specific thing can make the experience quite tiresome and the process difficult, because what is available in a thrift store is completely dependent upon people's donations. So rather than looking for a specific brand or style, use the variety of clothes as an advantage. It is also beneficial to search through the thrift stores often; what is available changes frequently and becoming a regular customer can score you some great finds. I visit my local thrift shops once every other week, or whenever I have an afternoon off, so I am always updated. Perhaps some people are hesitant to try thrift shops. The thought of wearing other people's clothes may perhaps feel uncomfortable, but there are many advantages to wearing pre-loved clothes. Newly produced garments are often treated with harsh chemicals, which affect both nature and your health. With pre-loved clothes, those chemicals are often long gone. When the clothes have less chemical residue, they are both more sustainable and healthier. Of course, there are some types of clothing that are easier or more comfortable to buy new, like underwear—and in that case, I would go and look for sustainable underwear brands, because I know there are plenty of them. However, other types of clothing, like shirts, pants, skirts, dresses, and outerwear, can be found in thrift shops, and shopping like this not only helps the environment, in most cases it is also much cheaper. If you buy the majority of your clothes secondhand for a fraction of the original price, there will often be room in the monthly budget for other sustainable investments.

When finding your way in a thrift shop, the easiest thing to do is to start in one corner of the store and work your way through all the clothes. Some pieces are sometimes misplaced, other styles are unisex, and even if you do not think there is anything for you in the men's/women's/children's section, take a look anyway; I've been pleasantly surprised before.

Clothing swaps and secondhand apps

However, secondhand clothes do not have to come exclusively from thrift shops; there are many other ways to shop pre-loved, like exploring flea markets of different kinds. Here, individuals can rent a space to sell stuff from their own homes, and I've often come across people selling various stylish shoes and clothing, some of it practically unused. I really like flea markets because the countless small vendors make finding a scoop very likely, especially when every vendor is different. Clothing-swap events can also be arranged among friends and family, or you can invite people from your school or workplace. Social media is a great tool when arranging these sorts of events, or for discovering events arranged by others in your local area. There is something truly great about "the hunt" when you are looking for great finds, and this way it's easy to make secondhand shopping a cozy spare-time activity without supporting fast fashion.

Moreover, you do not even have to leave your house if you want to do secondhand shopping. At this point, there are countless websites and apps that let you browse other peoples' wardrobes or check out new vintage stores. Examples of these apps and platforms include Depop and Thredup (and probably tons more), and it's much easier to look for specific styles on these apps than in physical thrift stores. They have great search functions that let you narrow down specific brands and styles if you are looking for something special. On these apps, you

can communicate with the people selling the clothes, and you can agree on a price and how you want it shipped to you. Whenever I'm buying secondhand like this, I always ask the people selling if they can ship plastic free, i.e., without unnecessary plastic bags and tape. However, even if your parcel comes wrapped in plastic, it still has a much lower impact than buying new fast fashion.

Repairs and Maintenance

We need to treat our clothes well because they are difficult to recycle. When clothes are discarded, they end up in incinerator plants being burned, or in landfills where even natural fibers will never decompose. By extending the lifetime of your clothes by one to two years, you can help reduce the impact of your clothing by up to 24 percent. This is done by being careful with your clothes, and by learning how to repair small damages like rips and cuts. Also, keep in mind that some materials are easier to repair than others. Cotton, for instance, is much easier to work with than synthetic materials like polyester, so there are more reasons, besides releasing microplastic, to opt for natural materials.

How we wash our laundry also plays a part in the maintenance of clothes, and if you want to know more, you can read the chapter about zero-waste laundry (see page 76). But when the clothes cannot be worn anymore, and there are no ways of fixing them, then it is obviously not just going in the bin. Natural materials like cotton can be cut into makeup remover wipes or tissues. Alternatively, they can also be made into kitchen clothes. The possibilities are endless, and the only limits are those of your imagination. Buttons and zippers can also be removed from the clothes and reused in DIY projects or donated to a thrift store.

How to make your clothes last longer:

- Wash them gently, and avoid using a dryer if possible.
- Only wash the dirty spots by hand if you spill something.
- Freeze your clothes overnight if they have a bad odor.
- Learn how to mend and sew.
- Choose quality materials that can easily be fixed.

Tips for the Minimalist Wardrobe

Your wardrobe does not have to be boring and grey just because it's minimalistic. You can always be inspired by the philosophy behind the concept of *capsule wardrobes*, where the few selected pieces in your closet reflect an essential core; this being necessity and quality rather than having a closet filled with clothes you practically never wear. You can always use this approach in all aspects of your life to reduce your impact to the most elementary and necessary components, however, when it comes to clothing, there are exceptionally many advantages to benefit from. A capsule wardrobe is simply all about reflecting upon what is necessary in your wardrobe and what is not. It is about getting a good overview and then removing the unnecessary parts. You can ask yourself, "Is it really necessary to own twenty-three T-shirts and eighteen dress shirts?" Because that is rarely the case. With a capsule wardrobe, you will experience fewer moments of dress-code despair and generally achieve a sense of clarity when it comes to style, because you have reduced your options so only the best parts remain. The average consumer also has tons of clothing in their wardrobes that they don't particularly like—clothing that does not fit well or which is never used because it's simply too fancy. By removing these components, you automatically create clarity. With wardrobe appreciation, it is of course also important to not throw away all the clothes that were deemed unnecessary. Instead, donate them to thrift shops or sell them. Owning less will often also come with a decreased need to buy new things; at least that is my personal experience. Creating a super-well-thought-out wardrobe also makes you appreciate simplicity and timelessness.

Another reason why we often end up buying new clothes is because many stores, as previously mentioned, change their selection up to fifty-two times a year. They do that to make us feel untrendy or inadequate, and thus buying updated styles and on-trend items will make us feel good again. However, a capsule wardrobe's focus is timelessness and versatility, which often comes with the avoidance of trends and short-lived styles. Dressing this way will also make you feel like you are one step ahead. Shopping can also become something like an addiction because it provides us with a quick sense of happiness, or a rush, which quickly fades—so finding other, more meaningful activities will help reduce the cravings for shopping trips.

Tips for a good capsule wardrobe:

- Only acquire clothes that fit you perfectly.
- Choose natural quality materials.
- Find your basics which can be used for both casual and formal occasions.
- Pick timeless over trendy.

Fashion Mentality and Designer Labels

When I was in high school, I cared a whole lot about what brands I was wearing. I could not afford designer clothes at all, but I perceived wearing designer goods as a positive thing—a thing that signaled success and wealth. The prestige surrounding designer goods is something most consumers are aware of, and when you think about it, it's actually quite a peculiar concept. Deep down, we know that just because there is a certain label on a handbag, that does not necessarily make that handbag better than others. Still, we tend to react differently to designer bags than we do to bags bought in the clothing section at a grocery store. There is, of course, more than just the one reason, but I think the symbolism of designer labels has a huge role to play in our perception of products. Even though the prestige of designer brands is completely made up, something about it is kept alive between us because of our reactions to and treatment of the products. The big designer brands spend millions annually keeping this fictional prestige alive through marketing campaigns

and advertisements, all curated to tell us that we will become better versions of ourselves with a designer bag across our arm. Thus, using designer brands comes to be about what we signal to the world around us. Collectively, we fall for it. It can be intensely difficult to distance yourself from the idea of prestigious brands, but, luckily, it's not impossible. The notion that finally made me cut my ties to the designer brands (or my perception of them; as I mentioned, I do not have the cash for this stuff, like at all) was quality. I have always had this idea that you pay thousands upon thousands of dollars for designer products because they are good quality, and, furthermore, that they are produced under good conditions, but sadly, that is far from the truth. Many big designer brands have their products produced in sweatshops, in completely the same way cheap fast-fashion goods are produced. The price you pay for a designer product is not necessarily an indicator of the quality, nor is it an indicator of fair wages or a sustainable supply chain. The price you pay is primarily used to keep the prestige of the brand alive. We pay to be told a story. It was incredibly disappointing to learn that many garment workers are paid the same low, unlivable salaries no matter whether they make a bag worth ten dollars or a thousand dollars.

In a similar fashion (pun intended), there is not necessarily a huge difference between the sustainable efforts made by big designer brands and those made by cheap fast-fashion clothing companies. Designer labels are not doing much to make their production of clothes more sustainable, and they release the same amounts of chemicals and dyes into water systems and generate just as much unnecessary waste as the fast-fashion stores (actually, designer labels often do not go on sale because that would weaken the value of the brand, so, instead of discounting or donating clothes that were not sold, they are thrown away and burned). Knowing the dirty secrets of designer brands, it didn't take long for me to lose interest in them after I stopped glorifying extravagant spending on designer goods. Today, I am not even the tiniest bit impressed by the amounts of money people spend on designer goods, and I will not be until the brands use their wealth to improve the supply chain, production, and general impact.

However, it can be difficult to change other people's opinions about expensive bags, shoes, and coats, especially if you are the only one around who changed their own perception of these products. Therefore, I have acquired secondhand ammunition: every time someone compliments my outfit, I always reply that it's thrifted or sustainably produced. Naturally, I also say thank you (I am not completely devoid of manners). Changing the perception of designer brands, and generally changing the way we perceive fashion, is all about pushing our fashion mentality and our consumer values in a sustainable direction. It has happened quite often that someone has said: "Wow, what a cute dress, that looks so great on you!" to which I reply: "Thank you so much, I actually got it in a thrift shop for next to nothing. Can you believe it?" In this exchange, it often happens that people interpret this as me being modest or embarrassed, and they think that I am trying to talk myself down. I have often gotten reactions like: "Oh no, you don't have to mention that. No one can see it." However, I genuinely do not regard secondhand clothes and second-tier fashion as "lesser," even though I can feel from people around me that they're much less impressed by what you find when looking through countless thrift shops for the right look. No, it is much more impressive to walk down to a department store and spend next month's rent so you can wear a fancy logo. Honestly, I do not see the appeal at all, especially not when we consider that globally we have produced so much clothing that, technically, we never have to produce new clothes again (at least, not if we didn't burn the ones that don't sell). When we buy new clothes, we create more demand for even more new clothes to be made, but we do not create any new demand when buying secondhand. So I will just keep "talking myself down" to remind people that you do not have to spend a thousand bucks to look like a million (also, I apologize for the clichéd nature of that sentiment, but you've got to agree that it was a perfect fit).

Materials and Textiles

It isn't completely irrelevant which materials you choose when shopping for clothes, whether what you buy is new or pre-loved. Some materials have significantly shorter life spans, some release microplastic particles, some require obscene amounts of resources to produce, and some may come with other ethical dilemmas. It is easy, as a consumer, to throw in the (organically produced) towel and not bother to further research the processes by which our clothes are produced. Perhaps you figure that it's downright impossible to make a sustainable decision, and perhaps your closet at home is already full of fast-fashion items, so why not just quit this eco-project? However, whenever it's time to replace something in your wardrobe, it's a good idea to have a grasp of which materials have what impact—based on that knowledge, you can then make an informed decision. In essence, that is what the sustainable lifestyle is all about: making decisions based on facts about the product, rather than letting convenience and habits dictate your purchases. So here is a list of some of the more common materials used in clothing and their impact.

Leather: Eighty percent of the world's leather production still uses chrome to tan the leather. Chrome is a metal that is quite toxic and pollutes the water systems in and outside tanneries. It also affects the workers who work in the factories because, in most cases of outsourced production, they're not supplied safety equipment. Sean Gallagher won a Pulitzer award for covering this in his documentary *The Toxic Price of Leather*, which is definitely worth a watch. Leather is made using skins from several types of animals, like crocodiles, kangaroos, goats, fish (yeah, fish!), and the most commonly known animals associated with leather production, cows. As we will also discover later in the book, the management of livestock, especially cattle, and the conventional and industrialized ways in which we are raising these animals today, cannot be performed in a sustainable way. This production is extremely polluting and impactful. Leather is usually a byproduct of an unsustainable industry that needs to be dismantled and defunded (the skin of a cow accounts on average for 10 percent of the cow's value), and because of this, conventional new leather products are not sustainable. However, there are also cases where the leather isn't a byproduct but rather the primary product. Various luxury brands produce leather using leather cattle, which are slaughtered primarily for their skins. This is also the case for reptile leather.

Secondhand leather and vintage leather can have certain advantages because the material in itself is extremely tough, it does not release microplastic, and it's easy to repair. If you want to use leather, the most sustainable choice would be to buy it secondhand so your purchase does not increase demand for new leather products. You can also support companies who use secondhand leather in their production of "new" products, or independent shops that re-tan old leather by using plants rather than chrome.

Vegan leather: With synthetic leather (or *pleather*), you avoid supporting animal agriculture and the polluting practices related to making leather. However, that does not necessarily mean that pleather is completely without impact. Some vegan leather products are made from plant-based sources like pineapple skins, apple leather, or cork, but most of it is still made from plastic. Specifically, plastic-based leather is often made from PVC, and that is a problem. PVC, or polyvinyl chloride as it's super elegantly called, is one of the most polluting types of plastic. The impact of a product made from synthetic leather is still smaller than the impact of a product made from animal-based leather. However, if you want to pollute as little as possible, I recommend going for plant-based leather options made from natural fibers rather than plastic. Especially if it is a product you're planning on wearing a lot (plastic-based material will release microplastic during washes and wear).

Fur: One of the materials I have most commonly seen advertised as sustainable is fur, and at first glance it also looks okay. Fur can last for decades and often breaks down in a compost. But the fur industry is far from sustainable. The production of fur is energy intense, polluting, and has huge consequences for biodiversity. Wastewater from mink farms result in nitrogen pollution in surrounding water systems, and many fur companies have outsourced their production (due to bans) to other countries with fewer environmental laws and restrictions. For instance, 90 percent of the fur produced in Poland is exported. Fur products are also treated with chemicals like formaldehyde, chrome, and ammonia, all of which affect the surrounding environment. Like animal agriculture, the fur industry also emits greenhouse gases and is dependent on fossil fuels—all to mass-produce products used for decorative purposes and for prestige. Notice how the general fur industry that I am referring to here is entirely different from the fur-consumption practices of indigenous peoples, which is an entirely different ballgame because it's neither an industry nor a case of mass production. The fur industry is kept alive by the prestige some consumers associate with wearing fur, usually in climates where it serves no necessary purpose. As a consequence, most consumers can easily survive and thrive without fur products. Of course, faux fur made from synthetic materials, a.k.a. plastic, has the same disadvantages as pleather, and thus, the most sustainable choice would be to avoid both.

Wool: When we think about wool, we often think of sheep—but wool also comes from rabbits, camels, goats, and llamas (angora, cashmere, merino, and mohair). Depending on the type of wool production and where that production takes place, the material's overall impact can vary quite a lot. Wool is often treated with fewer chemicals than fur and leather; however, wool production also comes with nuances that can be hard to figure out. Some types of wool production utilize organophosphates, which are corrosive phosphorus acids related to several types of chronic illnesses among factory workers. In organic wool production, the sheep, or other animals, often get to graze in places where food for people cannot be grown, and therefore organic wool production does not take up a lot of space that could have been used for more sustainable purposes.

However, in conventional wool production, the exact opposite is the case, which adds to the impact of the material. China is the third-biggest producer of angora wool (made from rabbit wool), and the supply chain is affected by both unethical treatment of the animals as well as energy-intensive factory practices. In conventional wool production, overgrazing often becomes an issue, and it leads to poor soil quality (which means that the soil cannot be used to grow crops of the same quality or quantity as before). Australian wool production, furthermore, utilizes *mulesing*, which is a technique that involves cutting off the skin around the anus of the animals to avoid ingrown wool and parasitic infection—this is often done without sedation. One would think that wool is more ethical than both fur and leather because the animals are not slaughtered for their wool, and to some extent that is true. It is, in that sense, more ethical, but many types of sheep and other animals used for wool production have, over time, been bred to produce unnatural amounts of wool. This is very painful for the animals because they become unable to move if they're not regularly cut. Therefore, there are ethical dilemmas related to supporting an industry that has bred animals into a state where they're dependent upon human interference to survive (the same is true of dairy cows and egg-laying hens).

However, wool also comes with advantages. It has antibacterial functions, which means that you do not have to wash wool products as often as other types of materials. It is also easy to recycle or compost. Despite these advantages, the most sustainable way of consuming it would be by buying it secondhand or finding an organic wool brand.

Cotton: This is a material which can easily be recycled, composted, or sewn into new products. It is also the most utilized material in the garment industry today, and because of this, it is especially crucial that we support the right kinds of supply chains and brands. As is perhaps obvious at this point, there are many advantages to be found when supporting organic materials, and cotton is certainly not an exception to that rule. Conventional cotton production is the world's largest consumer of pesticides and insecticides, both of which have fatal consequences for biodiversity, ground water, and cotton workers' health. About a thousand people die every day as a result of pesticide poisoning. The production of cotton accounts for 2.4 percent of global land use, but the industry consumes 18 percent of the world's pesticides and 25 percent of its insecticides according to the documentary *True Cost*. This is more than any other kind of agriculture. In

organic cotton production, these pesticides and insecticides are not
used, which makes the material less impactful on the environment
in which it's grown. Furthermore, organic cotton production is often
involved in other initiatives, like programs that protect biodiversity
and bee populations, which fulfill a social responsibility. Whether it's
conventional or organic, cotton production requires a lot of water.
Cotton is produced when large machines process cotton fibers,
a process which requires both energy and water. It takes about
710 gallons of water to produce one cotton T-shirt. In conclusion,
choosing organic cotton is way better for the environment, but
buying too much is still unsustainable, no matter how organic it is.
Buying only what we need is always the way forward.

What are the most sustainable materials?

It sounds like everything we wear is unsustainable and everything
we buy is bad. Yes, when production goes up but prices go down—
which is exactly what is happening in fast fashion—then there are
no sustainable ways of producing these clothes. In that sense, it's
all bad. However, that does not mean nothing can be done about it,
because, naturally, some things can. Initiatives and first-movers are
popping up everywhere with new sustainable production techniques
and new eco-friendly textiles; materials that keep the promises
they make and that don't only look green on the outside. It can be
a really good idea to support these initiatives as a consumer. But,
of course, it's a question of balance. Personally, I have found that a
20/80 solution works great for me. Twenty percent of my wardrobe
consists of new, sustainable brands, and 80 percent is secondhand.
Maybe you find another balance—that does not make it wrong or any
less valid. The most important thing to keep in mind is to reduce and
avoid conventionally produced materials and fast-fashion products.

Here is a list of materials which are widely recognized to be the most sustainable:

- **Recycled cotton** with a GOTS certificate: This ensures an ethical supply chain and no pesticide use. Recycled cotton is also better than new, organic cotton because it requires less water and is often made from fibers that would otherwise have been wasted.

- **Organic hemp** has been used for hundreds of years for textile production. Hemp requires very little water to produce, and the plant can grow in most places. Additionally, hemp also fertilizes the soil it grows in.

- **Organic linen** made from flax is a very versatile material. Flax can grow in many types of soil; it does not need a lot of nutrients to grow—and the entire plant is used, which means that nothing is wasted (kudos for being a zero waster!)

- **Tencel** (lyocell) is a synthetic-natural hybrid material based on wood fibers. It requires very little water to produce, and it can be recycled in a closed loop, which reduces waste and water pollution.

- **Pinatex** is one of the best types of vegan leather. It is made from pineapple leaves, which are otherwise thrown away when the pineapples are harvested.

- **Econyl** is a more sustainable alternative to nylon. Econyl is a product which recycles plastic materials in a closed loop and produces a nylon-looking product. Products made from econyl release fewer microplastic particles than normal nylon.

- **Qmonos** is a product inspired by spiderwebs. It is actually a type of synthetic silk which is completely biodegradable. It is better than nylon and stronger than steel; a rather badass material (and as a sustainable badass, you gotta love that!).

Chapter 8

Food and Grocery Shopping

The fact is, most people need more than simply reading a couple of numbers before they change their habits, even if they really want to. If change isn't something a person is welcoming, it instantly becomes a thousand times more difficult to achieve said change, or to even be inspired to make a change. This book is not necessarily meant to do all the work to change you; I surely hope you will put in some of the work yourself. This book is meant to give you the knowledge necessary to navigate consumerism and to prepare you to be a critical and conscious consumer so that you make the most sustainable decisions when you're in clothing stores, supermarkets, restaurants, bars, or on holiday. I want to inspire realistic and long-term changes, and that is done most efficiently by taking small steps every day. In my opinion, taking steps that are too big, expecting too much of yourself in too little time, or setting goals that are unrealistic will typically only inspire short-lived changes that will fade out once the dust settles. That is not a sustainable lifestyle change. The best way I can explain this is by telling you how I found my way to a plant-based diet (because that is something of a rollercoaster ride), and how I myself have navigated all this information that is constantly available, but somehow still unattainable, you feel? Okay? Okay.

I have always been infamous in my family for my appetite for meat, especially big steaks. Moreover, my love for meat, and the amounts I consumed, always created positive reactions from my family and friends. Throughout my upbringing, I have been socially awarded for making choices in my diet, and the more meat fifteen-year-old Gitte would put on her plate, the bigger were the smiles around the table. Now, while I, in the moment of writing this book, have been a vegan for three years, I retroactively see why it took me such a long time to reduce the amount of animal products I ate. Because food is more than fuel and the stuff we put in our mouths. Food has meaning—there is a cultural significance to food, and it can be difficult to reinvent your diet if you're the only one doing it. Food is more than the stuff that keeps us alive: it is a social minefield, and there are an excessive amount of emotions and traditions related to food. When excluding animal products, you have to confront those emotions and face them head on, especially if you're going all the way as a vegan. I would say it's all worth it, though.

When I started making videos and writing my blog about sustainability, I was still eating animal products. I went down to the local butcher shops with my mason jar and to the cheese shop with my stainless-steel container—that way I avoided all packaging. I was super proud of myself, so it really hurt when people online were criticizing me for my food choices. They asked questions and fired statistics in my direction which I had never seen before and which I was not in any condition to comprehend. I tried protecting myself by categorizing all of these comments as hateful bullying. Every time someone asked me, "Have you considered making a vegan recipe?" I saw it as a personal attack. I became very anti-vegan, and I actually made a video on my channel explaining why I would never go vegan. It didn't slow the critique down, by the way, and I ended up removing the video a couple of days later. Is this chapter going to be about how I was bullied by vegans, how they're awful, and how all of this was super undeserved? Nope, we're going to take another detour.

Slowly, I started to eat more flexitarian (I drastically reduced my meat consumption). However, the reactions from my surroundings were not necessarily supportive, so it was difficult to find safety in any form of diet. I spent a lot of time reading articles about veganism and I started having this bad feeling in my stomach every time I was out hosting zero-waste workshops. I felt dishonest because I knew I could do more, but the pressure of social codes and convenience held me back. At one point, I thought that enough was enough. I proclaimed myself a vegetarian. It created some stir around me, but the reaction I remember the most, and heard the most, was: "Luckily, you still eat cheese. That means you still get to live a little." I quickly got the impression that people did not want me to go any further than being vegetarian—they did not want to see me become "extreme" because there seemed to be this consensus that all vegans are judgmental extremists and people who bully you online (in a second, we're going to talk about animal agriculture, so some people might not see me as a total non-judgy vegan, but what can you do?). I had a really hard time being a vegetarian. I fell into "meat accidents" all the time, sometimes because of social pressure, but honestly, sometimes it was simply because I craved the comfort of the food that I denied myself, and this happened whenever I was sad or tired (and because the vegetarian dishes I made back then were super-duper boring).

However, suddenly something happened. I was going home from a night out with my friends, and I had had quite a few beers—in my own reusable cup to avoid plastic, of course. On the way over to the bus, I passed a Burger King, and I bought a chicken burger. I was in a mood that was very "Heck, no one is going to tell me what I can and cannot eat." I unwrapped the burger, but I simply could not eat it. Physically, I could not get myself to take a bite. Now, I will blame some of this behavior on the beer, but I started crying in the restaurant...like, ugly crying. Out of the blue, I was hit by the ethical aspects of veganism, all at once. I felt this extreme sense of injustice—why do we treat some animals like garbage while we buy jewelry for others? Who gets to decide all of this? Who gets to decide that this chicken's life was not worth more than the two dollars I spent on my burger? Now, I know this all sounds very emotional and soppy, perhaps even a little tree hugger-esque, but it started to make sense to me.

After that night, the feeling of injustice never left my body. I had always been a child who would befriend the ducks in the park. Here is a little fun fact: When I was twelve years old, I wanted to go vegetarian for a week, but it did not go as well as I had hoped because no one was there to help me back then. I retired this notion of being an animal friend because people liked me better when I was munching down on big steaks, so that is exactly what I did. But that severely drunken night at a Burger King in Aalborg, I felt like that girl again. This is a little sentimental and, for that, I am sorry, but this was a big milestone for me because it marked a very drastic shift in my perception of the world and how I fit into it. The reason I chose to tell you this story is to show you that not everyone's way toward refusing animal products is a straight line—it can be messy. The road to a more sustainable diet does not have to be perfect, and you might take some detours, but that does not matter as long as you move forward. I am not telling you to go get drunk on a Wednesday night and stubbornly force yourself to eat fast-food chicken burgers (I would not recommend that to anyone), but it taught me a very important thing. You cannot genuinely change just because you feel pressured into doing so. The only way to create long-lasting, sincere change is by asking yourself if what you are doing now is right and if you are acting according to the best of your ability. When we remove social codes, convenience, taste, and price, the questions become much easier to answer. The next section is filled to the brim with information that I hope you, as a consumer, can make use of in your everyday life.

Animal Agriculture

If you want to live a more sustainable and zero-waste life, you must look into and acknowledge the impact of those products and industries we surround ourselves with on a daily basis. Exactly like the impact of the fashion industry, it's not only the physical trash that ends up in our bins that we need to work on. Making green choices based on the entire impact of a product goes a long way and will always be more effectively sustainable than just focusing on the trash we can see. So this chapter will focus on the impact of animal products and how easy it can be to phase them out, why we need to phase them out in the first place, and what exactly to replace them with. It often feels like the best solution is to simply look the other way, and, especially if we are not really interested in food, this is probably also the easiest thing to do. But we did not show up to be sustainable badasses only to settle for easy solutions. If we did, this book would be a whole lot shorter. We are here because we're curious and because we want to know more about the products that we are spending money on, because we want to create good and green habits. A good step to take is to read this chapter about animal agriculture (perhaps that was not your first thought when you woke up this morning but, alas, here we are).

Fast facts about animal agriculture:

- 26 percent of our planet's available land is used for livestock.
- Another 33 percent of the world's available land is used to grow food for livestock.
- 7 percent of all emissions are caused by animal agriculture, which is more than cars, ships, and planes combined.

Many countries, my home country of Denmark included, are very proud of their agricultural industry and tradition, and there are many reasons for this. The industry of livestock, and agriculture in general, represents millions of jobs, and the animal products often represent long lines of tradition passed down for generations. That all sounds like a good thing, but there are other aspects of this industry that do not deserve sugar coating.

Livestock takes up around 80 percent of all land used for agriculture, specifically factory farming, yet it produces less than 20 percent of the world's supply of calories. Globally, there is actually enough cropland to feed more than nine billion people if we started using our agricultural space for food directly eaten by humans, rather than for feed for livestock. In Denmark, two-thirds of the country is used for intensive agriculture and 79 percent of what we produce is livestock. Meanwhile, 44 percent of the US is used for agriculture and a whopping 41 percent of US land in the contiguous states revolves around livestock. When wastewater from livestock is released into nature and water systems, it causes groundwater pollution and nitrogen pollution, both in salt and fresh water. One of the consequences brought about by this industry is more frequent oxygen depletion and extensive loss of biodiversity. Both flora and fauna in heavily farmed areas are affected by the industry and, sadly, very little is done to provide protection for wild animals and plants. Massive amounts of methane are released through animal agriculture. For instance, cows and the greenhouse gases they emit are directly related to the climate changes which we are globally affected by. On top of that impact there is deforestation, as the increased industry of factory farming needs more and more land cleared to grow food for their livestock. With the way we're producing animal products today, and the method by which most animal products are made, there is really no way of doing it sustainably.

In order to combat the impact of agriculture, we have to lower the demand for animal-based food production and transition into plant-based food production. It is necessary because the production of plant-based food for humans requires fewer resources and less energy than producing meat and dairy. The energy absorbed by animals through their food does not make it all the way to our dinner tables. Instead, it's used while the animal is still alive and released as methane. It requires circa eight pounds of grains to produce one pound of beef, and it requires four pounds of grain to produce one pound of pork. So if we were to transition the animal agriculture industry, and especially factory farming, away from producing vast amounts of food for animals and toward producing food for humans instead, we would be able to feed a lot more people. Actually, we would be able to fight world hunger, simply because we would be able to grow so much more food on so much less land.

Imported Feed

Furthermore, a lot of the feed that is fed to livestock isn't produced in the same country as the livestock. Factory farms all over the world import livestock feed from Brazil and Argentina, among other places. These countries have a significantly high production of soy, which is also used in European agriculture. More than 80 percent of the collective production of soy is produced as feed for livestock. The South American production of soy is increasing because more and more countries are producing and exporting more meat products. This development has resulted in deforestation and burning of rainforest areas in order to make room for more soy production. It can be difficult to include all the information available in just a small chapter like this because, trust me, there is so much more to dive into. Everything we know about pollution, biodiversity, groundwater, the atmosphere, and the entire planet shows us that we have to reduce factory farming as much as possible, and that message is kind of hard to deliver in a fun and quirky way. So I hope you will seek out information about this issue yourself as well; information about how this industry is shaping our perception of food and how it negatively affects our environment because, when it comes down to it, food is the most important issue.

Inspiration and documentation

- The Food and Agriculture Organization of the United Nations' brief about *Livestock and Landscapes*.

- The documentaries *Cowspiracy*, *Eating Animals*, *Earthlings*, *Forks Over Knives*, *The Game Changers*, and *Dominion*.

Zero-Waste Meat?

When I started my zero-waste journey back in 2015, I was still eating animal products. I fell into a pretty common trap of exclusively focusing on generating zero waste within my home, which became an almost symbolic practice of sustainability. Back then, I went to the cheese shop and the butcher's with my reusable containers and put my products in there to avoid using disposable plastic. The people in the shops were super kind to me and thought it was a fun idea—so there, a zero-waste shopping experience! I was really proud of this routine. However, polluting and waste is about more than what ends up in our bin. I guess, at this point, it's pretty common knowledge that plane travel is polluting—and it's not just because of the plastic-wrapped meals on the plane. It is the usage of fossil fuels that keeps the plane in the air that is to blame for the primary impact, even though we cannot see it with the naked eye. This means that you cannot make plane travel 100 percent sustainable by simply refusing the plastic-wrapped meal onboard. In a similar fashion, avoiding the packaging of meat products will not automatically make the product sustainable. The resources used in animal agriculture are much greater than those in plant-based agriculture because it requires more resources to keep animals alive than to keep plants alive. In spite of this, we do not get the majority of our nutrients from animal products. We waste a vast amount of resources producing products that, by themselves, cannot sustain us. This does not make sense when we need to think sustainably. Water is one of the resources required to produce animal products. According to the Water Footprint Network, producing one pound of beef takes circa eight gallons of water.

Pollution of farming happens via:

- **Nitrogen turnover**: A part of livestock manure is used as fertilizer on the fields and that releases nitrous oxide, a greenhouse gas 298 times more potent than CO_2.

- **Cow burps**: When livestock digest their food, they release methane—a greenhouse gas twenty-five times more potent than CO_2. Methane is also released from manure tanks and when flooding rice fields.

- **Deforestation**: When the industry of agriculture is expanding, natural habits often end up being destroyed to create more fields and more room for the industry. Trees and other plants in natural environments can store much more CO_2 than monocultures of cultivated crops. Furthermore, wild nature is also much more efficient at CO_2 turnover.

- **Lowland soils**: When bogs, lakes, and meadows are dried out to make room for fields for agriculture, the previously stored carbon is released and, when it comes in contact with oxygen, becomes CO_2, which is then released into the atmosphere.

What about White Meat and Fish?

You do not have to look far to find out that red meat in particular is bad for the environment, and the advice to skip it comes from many different sources, ranging from health professionals to sustainability advocates. Red meat typically accounts for all four-legged mammals in livestock, so cows, pigs, sheep, etc. Around the world, nearly 1.5 billion pigs, 300 million cows, and 500 million sheep are slaughtered every year. Livestock factories are one of the world's most polluting industries because it requires massive amounts of resources to breed and feed animals in the amounts which we're currently producing, so cutting out the most polluting types of meat is a really good idea. Actually, it was also the first correction I made when I started to aim for a more planet-friendly diet.

Unfortunately, there is no quick fix when it comes to sustainability. There is no one thing we can stop doing and then everything will be alright, it goes deeper than fast tips and easy hacks. One of the pieces of advice I frequently see is that you can simply replace red meat with light meat or fish if you want to live more sustainably. And, yeah, okay, I don't want to be the party pooper (yet, here I am), but light meat, like chicken and fish, has its own problems. Even though the production of light meat and fish releases less CO_2 and methane than pigs and cows, they are still rather impactful products compared to plant-based alternatives.

In times when sustainability is on everybody's lips, there is a lot of focus on our oceans and ocean health. We have to protect our oceans, and it's essential that we do so, but we always want to eat fish. The problem is that overfishing impacts most oceans today, and illegal fishing is an everyday occurrence all over the world. In fact, many fish and shellfish products imported to Europe and the US are related to illegal fishing practices. In Chapter 1, we went over plastic pollution in the ocean, and one of the biggest polluters of ocean plastic today is the fishing industry. Lots of fishing boats drop or leave behind their nets and other gear when they are done with their catch—the equipment left behind is also known as *ghost gear*. Furthermore, a large percentage of fish and shellfish are caught using bottom trawling. With this method, a long thick net is dragged across the bottom of the ocean, and it catches everything in its path. One of the main problems, besides ghost gear, is the amount of bycatch that comes with this method. All those animals caught in the net that are not fit for sale will be thrown back into the ocean dead or wounded.

Facts about bottom trawling

- Thirty-eight million tons of sea creatures are unintentionally caught every year. That is 40 percent of all fish caught worldwide.

- Forty to 50 percent of what is caught when bottom trawling is thrown back into the ocean, dead or wounded.

- Bottom trawling stirs up the ocean bed, affecting not only animals but all life in the oceans, ranging from plants to micro-organisms, bacteria, and corrals. This has affected more than twenty-two metric gigatons of land mass.

- The shark and ray population in areas affected by trawling is significantly reduced or completely wiped out.

What Should We Eat Instead?

Generally, humans are very attached to their traditions—this is
something that is true for most of us. In Denmark, where I come from,
we are very proud of our agriculture and our livestock, and because of
this, meat and dairy play a rather essential role around most holidays;
that is the case for many other countries as well, so perhaps you can
relate. As a result of our traditions with animal products, it can be
really difficult to phase them out because we have happy memories
with certain dishes that go all the way back to childhood. Likewise,
as a result of animal products' presence in our everyday lives as well
as during traditions and holidays, it can be extra difficult to picture
a life without them. So the next couple of pages will be dedicated to
guiding you through this sometimes-difficult transition. The guide
will also include tips on how to replace impactful ingredients with
more sustainable ones while losing neither the traditional mood
nor nutrition.

Commonly heard statements about animal products and some solutions

These are some of the statements I have had to listen to over and
over again, and my typical answers and explanations. For the purpose
of this exercise, I have actually teamed up with my good friend Stig
Ladefoed, who is a trained nurse with a certification in nutrition and
plant-based diet (in case you were thinking I was just coming up with
stuff to yank your chain).

"I cannot do without milk in my coffee."

Well, you don't actually have to. Some plant-based milks react better
with warm beverages than others, and some of them may start to

separate once they are exposed to high temperatures. Personally, I recommended oat milk if you want to avoid this mess. It resembles the feel of skimmed milk, but oat milk has the lowest carbon footprint out of all the options. If you want fattier options, you can go for soy milk or nut milks, which still have a smaller impact than dairy.

"Local meat is better than imported vegetables."

Actually, the transportation impact of goods only accounts for 10 to 12 percent of the average overall footprint. So animal products, even if produced more locally than most veggies, will still come with a higher impact. Exceptions to this can be greens like avocados, mangos, and papayas, which are often imported with airplane travel. But no need to worry, you can enjoy most vegetables, even if they are imported, knowing they carry a lower carbon footprint than meat products.

"If you do not eat meat, your diet will be lacking protein."

There is loads of protein in plant-based food. Actually, all proteins originate from plants, and they do not have to go through animals before we can benefit from them. There is plenty of protein in broccoli, legumes, beans, tofu, lentils, chickpeas, and I could keep going on and on. Here is what Stig has to say about proteins:

> It is the most widely spread myth that you will start lacking proteins in your diet if you cut out meat. The truth is that a protein deficiency is exceptionally rare among people who reduce or avoid meat in their diets, such as flexitarians, vegetarians, or vegans. So it is not something to be concerned about if you remember to get enough calories through a healthy and widely varied selection of plant-based foods.

"Without dairy you will not get enough calcium."

Okay, it is going to be a long read if we are going to go through all micro- and macro-nutrients (I'll let that be a topic for another day). But the notion that calcium only comes from dairy is false. You can easily get the amount of calcium you need in a day on a plant-based diet with simple food variation and balanced eating habits. You can find calcium in most collard greens, as well as in broccoli, soy, tofu, chickpeas, kale, and several types of nuts and seeds. The average estimate of necessary calcium intake in an adult is roughly one pound, and including several of these foods in your diet will provide you with more than enough calcium.

"I don't feel full without meat."

A part of this feeling is often more psychological than physiological. We expect our meal to be divided in three parts; one part carbohydrates, one part green, and one part protein (and maybe a fourth part just for gravy if you are Danish). Often, it's simply a question of getting used to having your meal look different than what you are used to; however, you should know that if you avoid meat in your dish, you should replace it with something else. It does not have to be a meat substitute per se, but simply something to take the meat's place so you will get enough calories. Therefore, remember to not just leave out the meat but to also, at the same time, find food replacements like lentil steak, falafel, bean pâté, or something else that can be used in a versatile way. Stig says:

> You can get full without meat. Several studies actually show that eating a plant-based meal on average leaves people feeling more full or satisfied than meals with meat. This is because of the high contents of fibers from whole grains, legumes, and vegetable fibers that are not found in meat—fibers both help increase and expand the feeling of being full.

"Replacement products and soy are far unhealthier than meat."

It can be quite a big change to replace all meat products with vegetables, beans, and nuts. So to make it easier, enjoying a soy or pea-based "replacement" meat product is a great alternative. They are often really handy and make it easier to have well-known dishes that usually require meat, just without the cholesterol, nitrite, and nitrosamines, and with less saturated fat. Even though meat substitutes contain less healthy plant components and nutrients, like fiber and antioxidants, in comparison to whole foods, they're still present in a smaller concentration. Therefore, there are still health-related advantages to replacing meat with soy or pea-based alternatives. A large analysis from 2018 also found that more than fifty thousand deaths a year can be avoided if more people gradually phase out meat in favor of plant-based replacements.

"I do not like the taste of replacement products."

It is also important to note that you do not have to eat replacement products and alternatives, like plant-based yogurt, cheese, milk, or "meat" to live greener—you can simply just avoid the animal products. However, it can also be a matter of getting used to something new. For instance, I really dislike soy milk, but after searching for a while, I found that oat milk has all my needs covered. If you don't like the taste of the products, you can also start by using them in cooking and baking. No one can taste the difference between vegan butter and dairy butter when it's used in a gravy—and I know this because I have been testing it on my family for years.

Even with all the information in the world, it can still be hard to change your diet from one day to another. It took me years, and even though I now wish I had done something sooner, you can't underestimate and devalue the time it takes to change, and that is okay. If you have a hard time finding out where to start, here are some good steps that can take you in a plant-based direction. Remember, it is the small daily actions that count, and it's healthy to try new things.

- **Skip beef and lamb.** These types of meat have the highest carbon footprint out of all of them, and it's a really good place to start if you're a sustainable food newcomer. It is a super important step.

- **Use plant-based milk, cream, and butter** in cooking and baking. You cannot tell the difference anyway and it's better for the planet, so really just a win-win.

- **Choose a dish without meat** when you're out, or visit a vegan restaurant and check out how the pros are doing it. It is fantastic inspiration, and it gives you a good idea of what vegan food can be like when prepared well.

- **Find some dishes that you love to cook,** that taste nice, and that don't require meat or dairy. It can be really helpful to have positive experiences with green food and let yourself build positive associations with it.

Sustainable Lunches

Let us talk a little bit about packed lunches, since we actually use a considerable amount of unnecessary packaging bringing our food to work or school every day. There are simple and easy habits one can develop which will save a lot of pointless plastic. Packed lunches are usually synonymous with a lot of single-use products like plastic bags, tinfoil, cling film, and sandwich paper. This chapter will give you some tools to help you prepare a nice, packed lunch completely waste free.

Wax wrap

This is a nice alternative to tinfoil and cling film. You can heat it up by hand and the wax will shape itself to the content. After each use, the wrap is simply washed in warm water and left to dry on a rack. A single piece of wax wrap can be used for years if treated correctly. Many different types of wax are used for wax wraps, but I prefer the type made with soy wax. These wax wraps can be bought on various webshops or can be made at home.

Lunchbox

If you don't already have a lunchbox, you can easily find one in most secondhand stores or you can buy a metal lunchbox. Steel lunchboxes can last for decades, and should they eventually break, they can be recycled. However, steel lunchboxes are not always completely watertight, so they should only be used for dry goods.

Glass jars

A normal, recyclable glass or mason jar works as well as a lunchbox. It is designed to be watertight and is therefore well suited for wet foods. Mason jars or jars with flip-tops can usually be found in secondhand stores, so you don't even have to buy anything new. If the jars are smelly from whatever was recently in them, they can be washed with vinegar and left to dry in the sun for a day.

Canvas bags

A canvas bag can serve many functions and one of them is as a floppy lunchbox. Dry foods, like a sandwich, can be wrapped in a canvas bag and secured with a piece of twine tied into a knot. If the bag gets too dirty from this, it's easily washable, either by hand or in a normal laundry load.

Water bottles and canteens

Many water bottles are often made of plastic, and even though bottles are reusable products, they will eventually end up in the same way as disposable plastic when they're thrown out. If you need to buy a water bottle, you can look for alternatives in stainless steel or reclaimed aluminum, since they can be recycled. If you already have a water bottle, no matter the material, you ought to use it instead of buying a new one. You can also use an upcycled glass bottle. This works well for adults, but older children can also learn to use one if they take care not to break it. It is, of course, better to have a reusable container for drinks than to rely on juice or milk cartons, as these come in Tetra Paks and are unrecyclable. If you want something other than water on the go, you can always mix it in your own container from home.

Cutlery

If you need cutlery for your lunch, the easiest zero-waste solution is simply to bring your own from home. If you instead eat at a buffet-style canteen, it might still be a smart idea to bring your own cutlery if the canteen only provides disposable options. Bring a canvas bag or a napkin to wrap the used cutlery in afterward.

Your own box for salads

I have been in this situation hundreds of times: lunch at work or at
school is a "make-your-own-salad" affair, where you mix the salad
in either a plastic box or on a disposable plate. Not very zero waste.
In situations like that, I try to prepare from home and bring my own
container. In some cafeterias, you weigh the food to determine
how much you need to pay, and in these instances the container is
weighed before I start loading up the food, and then the weight of
the container is subtracted at the end. It usually helps if you give the
lunch staff a bit of a smile and explain what you are doing while they
weigh your food.

Snacks

I sometimes like to eat a little bit between meals, and I have found
an easy way to do that without generating waste. If you simply make
sure to pack your smallest container with some sweets or nuts, then
you avoid buying the same plastic-wrapped snacks from stores or
canteens. You can also just bring a piece of fruit, as these are plastic
free and any packaging is compostable (looking at you, banana).

Bringing Your Own Container— A Guide to Politeness

"Is it okay if I use my own container?" This is a sentence which, to
many people, can seem a little daunting, and I truly get why. There
are so many situations where we use disposable containers every
day: coffee to-go, popcorn at the movies, pick-n-mix candy during
the weekend, doggy bags from restaurants, hummus from the
deli, salad bars at the canteen, and the list goes on and on. That is

why it's a great zero-waste tip to simply bring your own container. I have already mentioned this a couple of times, and I will probably mention it more before the end of the book, so I thought it would be a good idea to talk about how to do this—especially if this is your first time doing it.

There are a couple of different solutions which fit different situations. If I am grocery shopping and need bread or candy, I usually don't need to ask for permission to use my own bags—I just do it and then explain what I have done once I reach the cashier. With pick-n-mix candy, I gladly pay the extra money that the weight of my cloth bag incurs (I am a big spender like that). I usually also wrap bread from the bakery section in a cloth bag, but I make sure to do so openly, making it clear that I'm not trying to steal myself a free baguette—that would reflect very poorly on the zero-waste community.

If I have to interact with an employee or staff member before I buy the product, I always ask for permission before using my own container. Last time I was at the movies, I used my own water bottle for soft drinks instead of the cinema's paper cups. In a situation like that, it's a good idea to have a container with measurements on it, so the cashier can see that I'm not trying to hustle my way to extra sugar water. If I don't have a container with measurements, I usually bring a container that is smaller than the disposable ones provided (again, big spender, y'all). When asking the employees for permission, it's important to have an open and positive attitude; be friendly, make eye contact, and, if necessary, explain why you want to use your own container. Tell them it's a clean container and that it will only be touching the things you are buying.

But what if they say no? Well, I have only ever been told no twice since I started doing this (though, mentally, I always prepare for it), and if you should hear no, there are three ways to deal with it. You can rationalize with the employee; explain the situation again, showing them that the container is clean, and even let them put the food in the container for you if it's a question of hygiene; and last but not least, you might be dealing with an employee who has been specifically told not to allow the use of foreign containers, and if that is the case, it does not do any good getting angry at someone who is just doing their job. In that situation, the best thing you can do is be friendly and wish them a good day. That has only happened to me once, and when it did, I managed to get a hold of the manager and explain the situation to them. I think they might have been so fed up with me at that point that I only got my way so I would leave the store—but hey, it worked.

Chapter 9

Kitchen Guide

I am there for good, sustainable, and versatile ingredients that you can use in a wide range of recipes. Those types of ingredients are super great and green, because it's far better to buy one thing with multiple purposes than to buy ten different ingredients you will not finish anyway. Not everyone has a nifty zero-waste bulk store just around the corner, so we often have to attempt low-impact shopping in conventional supermarkets. But it's possible to avoid a lot of waste in your everyday shopping, even though you don't have access to a bulk store. I actually made this into a series on my channel, where I made it my goal to go to normal grocery stores and see what the plastic-free options were. I then prepared a meal, or several meals, with the ingredients I found—so it is possible to do something, you just have to know what to look for.

Useful and Plastic-Free Ingredients to Have in the Kitchen

Oil: Many types of oil and vinegar often come in glass bottles and can be found in cold-pressed and organic varieties. Oils can be used both in hot and cold dishes, as well as for baking (and in makeup products, but more on that on page 207). Therefore, oil in a glass bottle is a great thing to always have in the kitchen.

Oats: These can also often be found in cardboard or uncoated paper. Some types of packaging have a shiny, thin layer of plastic on the front, so it's best to avoid those since they cannot be recycled. A carton of oats is one of my favorite staples to have in the kitchen because it's great for porridge, baking, and homemade oat milk, and it fills you up quite nicely. Homemade oat milk can be used in baking, on top of cereals, and in smoothies, so a carton of oats will get you really far.

Beans: You can often find beans in aluminum tins, and those are easy to recycle. Make sure to avoid some of the cheaper brands if you can, as some of them contain BPA—picking a brand that does not use that in their packaging is better (it often says so on the side of the tin). Beans can also be bought in bulk in health shops, and they're an efficient source of protein. You can boil them, mash them, blend them, fry them (put them in a stew). Bean patties, hummus, and chili sin carne are some of my favorite ways to use beans. In my kitchen, we prefer kidney beans, black beans, and chickpeas.

Potatoes: Indeed, a true classic which can often be found without packaging in normal supermarkets, potatoes are one of those foods that, when grown locally, have the lowest carbon footprint, so I often choose them over rice or pasta. Potatoes can also be used on pizza, as a fried snack (obviously), in salads, or in curry dishes. I often end up making my curries or chilies too spicy, and adding some small cut-up potatoes will neutralize some of the spice to make it more fitting for consumption—just a pro tip.

Lasagna sheets: Most pasta comes in plastic bags, and even the pasta that comes in cardboard boxes often has a small plastic window so the pasta can peek out, which is not amazing. However, lasagna sheets can often be found in plastic-free packaging, like cardboard boxes, with no windows—and they can be used for lots more than just lasagna. When

I am making my cashew carbonara and curry pasta salad, I crack up lasagna sheets into smaller pieces, and it's also a massive hit with friends and family.

Squash/zucchini: A vegetable that I have had a lot of luck with when it comes to plastic-free shopping. It is often available package-free in normal supermarkets, and it is a great addition to many dishes. I often shred it finely and add it in stews, curries, or in my bean patties. The squash will be reduced significantly when exposed to heat, so there are really lots of opportunities to add a lot of fiber to a dish this way.

Seasonal Greens

Seasonal greens, no matter if they're bought from the farmer, grown in your backyard, or bought in the grocery store, will always have a lower carbon footprint than greens that are grown in greenhouses or imported from other places in the world. Seasonal greens also tend to come with less packaging than many imported goods, most likely because they do not have to travel as far. Because of this, using seasonal greens is a great step on the road to eating better, healthier, and more sustainably. But when is something in season? Of course, this varies a lot depending on what part of the world you are in (and making a list for every nation would take up too much of this book).

However, fruits and veggies are not always the best environmental choice just because they are grown nearby. In intensive agriculture, we grow many different foods all year around that could never grow outside of greenhouses. For instance, in some North European supermarkets, it is actually better to buy imported tomatoes from Spain when they're in season than to buy local tomatoes from a greenhouse. That is because maintaining and powering a greenhouse requires a lot of energy—much more than it takes to transport tomatoes from Spain to, for example, Denmark. In fact, only 10 to 12 percent of a product's overall footprint comes from transportation emissions, provided it is not transported by plane.

Food Storage

To get the most out your groceries, it is essential that you store them correctly. When some goods are stored incorrectly, it can affect the longevity of the item. So it is a good idea to know exactly what to do with veggies and fruits when storing them— that way, you will throw away less food and get the most out of your groceries.

In and out of the fridge

When it comes to food storage, I have several methods. Produce like potatoes, onions, garlic, and carrots are kept outside the fridge, in a place without direct sunlight. Tomatoes stay fresh the longest if they are kept outside the fridge as well, and storing them cool will make them less flavorful. However, if I have some

tomatoes that are overripe, storing them in the fridge will buy an extra day or two so that there is time to eat them. I have seen many different solutions when it comes to storing leafy greens, and several experts will advise you to store them in plastic bags, as it will make the greens stay fresh and crisp for longer. However, in my experience, that isn't the case. So I place my leafy greens with the stalks in a jar of water inside my fridge. Greens like kale, spinach, parsley, and chives thrive in that environment and stay fresh for more than a week in some cases. Other types of greens, like lettuce, are left loose in the fridge drawer where they usually stay fresh for three to six days depending on type and temperature, but it is always enough time for me to eat them. If there are things in your fridge that you want to stay fresh for a long time, I would recommend placing them in the middle of the fridge because the temperature in the middle is cooler than both the top and the bottom. Unopened tins are kept outside the fridge, but if the tin is opened, the contents can still stay good for a couple of days in the fridge—I just cover the tin with some wax paper.

The freezer

It isn't difficult at all to use a freezer while avoiding the use of plastic. I often meal prep and make bigger portions for several days (not always on purpose) and then I save it in my freezer. It is tradition during the holidays that I make vegan holiday food, so during December, I make many small portions and freeze them until I need them. It is quite nifty for holiday dinners with friends  and family that you don't need to make everything from scratch, time and time again (I always have an emergency solution when it comes to plant-based options for parties, but more on that later).

If you want to freeze food without wrapping it in plastic, there are several things you can do. I often use a mason jar or an off-brand glass jar from the grocery store because I have tons of them anyway, so I might as well use them. Firstly, make sure both the food and the jar are at room temperature before freezing. Also make sure that you don't fill the jar all the way up; save about two inches of space in the top. This way, the content will have room to expand once it freezes. If there is no room, the content will expand anyway and break the glass. You can also use metal containers or wax paper. I have also seen many people store their compost in a paper bag in the freezer until it can be composted. This is an option if you do not have your own compost but rather use a public compost bin or someone else's private bin.

Food Waste

It is a great idea to compost your food waste, but there are also several small, clever hacks that you can apply to your daily life to make sure that you only have to compost the unavoidable. About 50 percent of all food produced ends up in the bin. A lot of it is thrown away before ever landing on the shelves in the supermarket, but a lot of food is also unnecessarily wasted in our own homes. To avoid this, there are many small things we can do to improve ourselves and learn how to keep our bins lighter. These are some of my favorites:

Kitchen scrap broth: When I prepare my veggies, like potatoes, onion, broccoli, carrots, etc., I always save the peels, stalks, and skins and put them in a jar in my freezer. These scraps are amazing when making veggie broth. "Waste" products like onion peels have so much flavor in them that it is a shame to throw them away. Therefore, it is better to freeze them until you have the time to make the broth. Broccoli stems can be boiled and blended with other vegetables to make a rich soup, whereas other scraps, like peels and skins, can be removed and composted when all the flavor has been cooked out into the broth.

Jam/syrup: When I am peeling carrots and apples, I also save the peels and cores. Boil the peels from four to five apples and five to seven carrots with two ounces of water and 3.5 ounces of sugar, as well as cinnamon, vanilla, ginger, or whatever flavors you like. Simmer for fifteen to twenty minutes and then let it cool. Lastly, run it through a food processor until all chunks have been blended. Then you have a great anti-food-waste jam.

You can also skip the blending step and separate the syrup from the peels. The peels are great in smoothies and the syrup is great on top of pancakes or in other baked goods.

How to Buy Groceries without Any Trash

It can be difficult to give exact and concrete tips on how to avoid waste like, "Just go there and buy this," because our shopping options and the selection of groceries available to us are not universal. They vary from country to country—heck, they vary from neighborhood to neighborhood. Because of this, I think the most efficient thing to do is share how I do my own personal shopping. I hope that you will be able to recognize some of the possibilities in stores near you, and furthermore, I hope that you will start looking for sustainable shopping hacks beyond what I describe. There is no one true and correct way of going about it. There is seldom one shop that can cover all your needs, and no matter where you live, or what your budget is, there are small things we can do to shop more sustainably. Also, do not feel completely discouraged if you cannot shop completely without trash; we are not always 100 percent successful in our efforts to live with zero waste, especially not in a society that isn't designed for zero-waste living. We all have an impact, and we all leave waste behind us. The zero-waste lifestyle is simply about the conscious decisions that lead to reevaluating how we use products, resources, and services—and with conscious consumption, a reduction of waste often comes naturally. With this mindset, we can get really far, and honestly, reducing waste can end up feeling like a secondary hobby, whereas trash avoidance feels like a sport. No kidding, it can actually be quite entertaining.

Easy swaps for the kitchen

- cotton kitchen cloths
- dish brushes in metal, flax, and wood
- a solid soap bar, or liquid soap from bulk in glass containers instead of plastic
- a compost bin for food scraps
- cleaning sponges in natural fiber
- reusable containers for leftovers
- wax wraps or fabric for sandwiches

Conventional Supermarkets

The majority of consumers do not, at this moment in time, have access to bulk shops and farmers markets (if you do, then go use them, seriously!). Most consumers have to settle for conventional grocery stores, but all zero-waste hope isn't lost. When I go shopping in a supermarket, I also do so without a shopping list. I look around and pick out the produce and other products I can find without any plastic, and then I adjust the rest of my shopping based on the plastic-free stuff. I always start out with fruit and veggies. In many grocery stores, you can find a solid selection of seasonal greens and locally produced goods, a lot of which are unwrapped. Of course, it can vary depending on season and store, but the produce I often have luck finding without plastic is stuff like cauliflower, potatoes, onions, spring onions, squash, peppers, cabbage, tomatoes, fennel, and, of course, several types of fruit. Perhaps you cannot find the same types of greens near yourself, or perhaps you're able to find much more. No matter what, basing your shopping on what is available plastic-free is a really good starting point. Fruit is often quite plentiful in the unpackaged departments, and some is even locally produced. I have had my luck finding local apples unwrapped, as well as imported goods like mangoes, passion fruit, and avocados. However, depending on where you live, if these goods have been imported from far away, I would advise you to not consume them as an everyday occurrence. They are quite resource intensive to produce and are often transported by plane, but we will return to this topic later.

Many of the larger supermarkets have a baking section where you can buy different sorts of baked goods package free. Simply bring your own bag (I recommend a mesh bag so the cashier can see what is inside). I have also encountered delicacy sections in larger shops where you can get hummus, olives, pickled onions, garlic, and salads in your own container rather than in plastic boxes—just remember to clean it really thoroughly before bringing it. It is also becoming increasingly popular for supermarkets to have bulk sections with nuts and seeds, and those can easily be a handy zero-waste snack on the go. When buying wet foods, it can be difficult to find bulk and refill options in many supermarkets—I have, personally, only seen a few. The next best thing is therefore to choose products that come in glass or metal containers (if those materials are included in your local recycling programs). Glass, as we know, can be recycled forever, and furthermore, glass is also easily upcycled in your home. You can find oil, juice, lemonade, wine, fizzy drinks, vinegar, and dressing in glass bottles.

Dried goods, like pasta, rice, flour, oats, etc., usually can't be found in package-free varieties in normal grocery stores, but the next best thing is untreated and uncoated paper and cardboard packaging.

However, be aware that some cardboard packaging is actually Tetra Pak, a type of packaging consisting of several layers of cardboard and plastic foil that typically cannot be recycled with paper (indeed, often it can't be recycled at all). Juice and milk cartons are often made from Tetra Pak.

With paper packaging, it is easy to fall for some easy marketing, and it has happened to me before (and, heck, it will probably happen again): a new product is launched in what appears to be packaging made from a paper box, however, once you look inside, everything is wrapped in plastic. To avoid this, the "shake test" can often uncover which boxes contain plastic inside and which ones do not. Simply put the container to your ear and give it a shake: Does it sound like the product rolls around loose in there or can you pick out some plastic crackling sounds? Spices can also be tricky to find without plastic, and unless you live close to a bulk store, this is one of the times where we often have to compromise our zero-waste ideals. You can find spices in small metal tins or glass containers, both of which are often sealed with a small piece of plastic, but it is certainly better than buying spices in plastic bags. There are also certain items that, in my experiences, are impossible to find plastic-free—at least at this point in time. In those cases, we have to think about how necessary these products are and make decisions on whether or not to buy them based not only on convenience and price but more so on necessity and functionality. Potato chips are a good example of a product that is unlikely to be found in packaging that is friendly to zero-waste efforts, but they can be replaced with other snacks like baked goods, nuts, or bulk sweets. In other situations, the complete opposite can be the case. If there are no means of getting foods like leafy greens without plastic, it might be worth compromising your zero-waste ideals, as these foods contain important nutrients that you need to thrive. It would be bad to entirely exclude some healthy foods from your diet because of their packaging.

Sometimes we consumers will run into products that are so grossly overpackaged that the packaging no longer serves any practical function. The best thing to do is, of course, to avoid buying those products. In the summer of 2019, I saw several supermarkets selling quarters of watermelons in foam trays, wrapped in eight to ten layers of plastic, and those trays annoyed me more and more each time I went into the store. However, it is often quite unconstructive to walk around being slightly pissed off at a supermarket, and it is actually helpful to the supermarket, the company, and yourself to simply communicate your complaint to those responsible. The more consumers who pressure the shops and the companies to rethink their packaging, the more likely it is that we can get them to change. And, of course, it also helps your mood significantly to voice your concerns rather than simply internalizing them unconstructively.

My Favorite Recipes

Birthday Buns

For eight people

You can easily make delicious, soft, and airy buns without animal products. I love this recipe, and originally I got it from my good friend Louise (a tiny shout-out because she really knows how to bake and, honestly, it inspires me to up my game on the daily). The buns are very nostalgic for me because they taste exactly like those my grandmother used to make for birthdays when I was a child.

Ingredients

- 2½ cups plant milk
- 2 oz of fresh block yeast (or ½ oz of active dry yeast)
- 1 tablespoon sugar
- 1½ teaspoon salt
- 1 teaspoon cardamom
- 6 cups white flour
- 6 oz vegan butter or margarine

Heat the plant milk until lukewarm and dissolve the yeast. Add sugar, salt, and cardamom. Add the flour little by little—here it can be an advantage to use a food processor, but it can also be done by hand. The butter needs to be soft when it is added but not completely liquid. Add more flour; again, little by little. Now knead the dough for at least 5 to 8 minutes but more is also great. Then place the dough under a clean kitchen cloth and let it rise for 1½ hours. When the dough is done rising, knead it again and divide the dough until the buns are roughly two-by-two inches. Place the buns on a baking tray and let them rise again, this time for 30 minutes. Afterward, you can give them an oil or milk wash and bake them at 350 degrees Fahrenheit in a preheated oven for 8 to 12 minutes. Take them out when they are golden brown and let them cool (just a bit) before digging in.

Burger Buns

6–8 buns

Ingredients

- 1 cup oat milk
- 1 oz of fresh block yeast (or ¼ oz active dry yeast)
- 1 teaspoon sugar
- ½ teaspoon salt
- ¼ cup olive oil
- 1 cup durum flour
- circa 1 cup wheat flour

Warm the oat milk on low heat until lukewarm. Then pour the oat milk into a bowl and add yeast and sugar. Stir until dissolved. Then add salt, oil, and durum flour. Add the wheat flour a little bit at a time until you can knead the dough with your hands. Cover a clean, smooth surface in flour and knead the dough for about 5 to 10 minutes. Then cover the dough with a clean kitchen towel and let it rise for 30 minutes. Knead the dough again

for 3 to 5 minutes and then divide it into 6 to 8 burger buns. Roll them smooth on the floured surface and let them rise underneath a cloth for 30 minutes again, this time on the baking tray. Then give them an oil wash and sprinkle with sesame seeds. Bake them for 8 to 10 minutes at 425 degrees Fahrenheit in a preheated oven, until they are golden brown.

Vegan Meringue

For eight people

You do not need egg whites to
make meringue—who would have
thought? All you need is the water
from chickpeas. You know, the
water that we pour down the drain
and never, ever use? Yes, that
water. This stuff is called aquafaba
and it's a super versatile ingredient,
and it's also pretty zero waste.

Ingredients

- **water from 2 cans of chickpeas**
- **2 cups sugar**

Pour the water from two cans of chickpeas into a pot and simmer for
10 minutes. Of course, save the chickpeas for some falafel or a good
curry—we're about zero waste here, dang it! Now, let the aquafaba
cool down and pour it into a bowl. Mix with circa 2 cups of sugar and
whisk for at least 5 minutes. The good thing about vegan meringue is
that you cannot whisk it too much, which is an issue when using egg
whites. You can therefore keep whisking until the texture is the way
you want it. You can use the aquafaba on ice cream, which is a huge
hit in my house. You can also make a crispy meringue by drying the
aquafaba for 1½ to 2 hours in an oven set to 25 degrees Fahrenheit.
The recipe I most often use the aquafaba for is a fresh pavlova with
seasonal fruit and vegan ice cream. I have made it with an oat-milk-
based vanilla ice cream, Danish Ingrid-Marie apples, bulk nuts, and
the anti-food-waste syrup from earlier.

Carrot Cake

For eight people

Ingredients

- 6 oz of sugar
- 4 oz of vegan butter or margarine
- 2 finely shredded carrots
- 2 teaspoons cinnamon
- ½ teaspoon ginger
- ½ teaspoon ground cloves
- ½ teaspoon salt
- 1 teaspoon vanilla
- 1 teaspoon baking powder
- 2 pints of plant milk
- 1 cup white flour

Preheat your oven to 350 degrees Fahrenheit. Mix sugar and butter with a whisk or in a food processor. Now turn the finely shredded carrot into the mixture and add spices, salt, vanilla, and baking powder. Add the plant milk (I prefer oat milk) and the flour, a little bit at a time. Mix thoroughly.

Coat the inside of a springform pan with oil or vegan butter and pour in the batter. Bake the cake for 15 to 20 minutes or until the cake is firm and golden brown. This carrot cake is great as a standard recipe to which you can add your own twist. You can easily add squash or beets as well. The first time I made this, I made two cakes, one slightly smaller than the other, and I added cocoa to one of them. Then I placed them on top of each other and topped them off with the aquafaba meringue and caramelized nuts. The result is a tall, festive cake that can be used as a birthday cake or for other celebrations and special occasions.

Homemade Oat Milk

2–3 pints

Out of all the plant milks that are available and used as more sustainable alternatives to dairy milk, I personally think that oat milk is the best option. Moreover, it actually has the lowest carbon footprint out of all plant-based milks, and of course, it has a lower footprint than dairy milk as well. At this point, plant milks are pretty accessible in many supermarkets, but did you know that it's super easy to make yourself? That way you always avoid some plastic or Tetra Pak packaging.

Ingredients

- ½ cup oats
- 2–3 pints of ice-cold water
- 1 bowl or glass jar to contain it

Blend the oats and the ice water at high speed for no longer than 15 to 20 seconds. It is important that the water is as cold as possible, otherwise the oat milk will turn out slimy. For the same reason, you

must not blend for longer than 20 seconds, otherwise the milk will start to heat up in the blender and, again, turn out slimy. After you have blended, run the milk through a cheesecloth, a clean kitchen towel, or a sieve. The fewer oat fibers that end up in your milk, the smoother the milk becomes. However, you do not have to throw away the oat pulp once you're done straining. I always add it in baking recipes or in pancakes where they completely dissolve into the batter. Oat milk can be used in cooking, in smoothies, in coffee, on top of granola, or on cereal (generally, it can be used for all the same purposes as dairy milk). This recipe can also be used when making milks from nuts; the nuts simply have to soak in water overnight, but otherwise the method is the same. You can make the milk thicker by adding less water or more oats if you want to make a cream-like product instead.

Green Ravioli with Nut Filling

For two people (or one hungry person! I am not judging)

Ingredients

- ½ cup olive oil
- 1 handful of fresh parsley
- 1 handful of fresh spinach
- 1 handful of wild garlic
- 1 handful of fresh basil
- 5 oz of wheat flour
- 5 oz of durum flour
- ½ cup water
- ½ cup cashews
- 2 teaspoon shredded nutmeg
- salt and pepper
- 2 tablespoons nutritional yeast
- juice of 1 lemon

Take half of the olive oil and blend it with your herbs in a food processor. Set it aside and start to work on your pasta dough. Mix the two types of flour and add water and your herb oil, as well as some salt (save some of the herb oil for the filling). Mix the dough with a fork and, when the dough starts to feel firm, use your hands to knead it together. Here you are using the warmth from your hands to set the dough. When it feels elastic but firm, set it aside to rest while you work on the filling.

Take the other half of the oil and blend it with the cashew, nutmeg, salt, pepper, nutritional yeast, and the last bits of the herb oil. The filling should start to look like a smooth paste after 1 to 2 minutes of blending. When you are satisfied with the consistency, set the filling aside, preferably in the fridge.

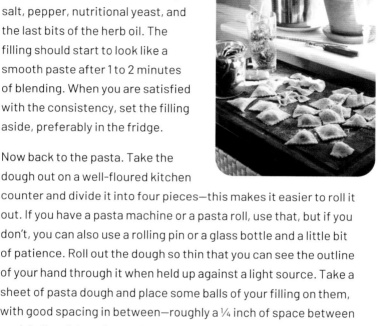

Now back to the pasta. Take the dough out on a well-floured kitchen counter and divide it into four pieces—this makes it easier to roll it out. If you have a pasta machine or a pasta roll, use that, but if you don't, you can also use a rolling pin or a glass bottle and a little bit of patience. Roll out the dough so thin that you can see the outline of your hand through it when held up against a light source. Take a sheet of pasta dough and place some balls of your filling on them, with good spacing in between—roughly a ¼ inch of space between each ball and the edge of the pasta sheet. When the sheet is full, coat the empty space on the pasta sheet with a little bit of water and then place another sheet of pasta on top. Make sure to gradually press out all air while you lay down the sheet, so that the ravioli will cook evenly and not break. When the top sheet is on, mark out where you want to make your cuts by using a chopstick to press down around the ravioli, then take a pasta cutter, or a knife, and cut them out. Remember to cover them in a thin layer of flour to avoid them sticking to each other (moisture is the enemy of uncooked pasta!). Bring salted water to a boil and cook the raviolis for 1 minute. Then take them out with a sieve and make sure to get as much water off them as possible, then serve with salt, pepper, and lemon juice.

Plant-Based Pasta Carbonara

For two people

Ingredients

- 1 cup chopped onion
- 2–3 cloves of garlic
- olive oil
- 4–5 dried lasagna sheets
- circa 1 cup homemade oat milk
- salt and pepper
- 2 tablespoons nutritional yeast
- ½ cup chopped fresh parsley
- 2–3 teaspoons ground nutmeg
- lemon juice

Start by browning the onion and garlic with olive oil on a pan on medium heat. Bring salted water in a pot to a boil, and once the water is boiling, add the lasagna sheets. I like to break them up into two to three pieces each. Remember to save the pasta water; it is filled

with starch that we are going to use in the sauce. When the onions are golden, little by little add oat milk, salt, pepper, yeast, parsley, and nutmeg. Stir until well mixed. Control the consistency by letting the oat milk reduce to a thick sauce and add pasta water to adjust. Lastly, add lemon juice for acidity. When the pasta is done cooking, turn them over in the sauce on the pan before serving. Enjoy with bread or a side salad.

Mac 'n' Tease

For four people.

One of my favorite dishes to serve, especially to guests who are slightly skeptical toward vegan food, is a plant-based version of mac 'n' cheese. I call it mac 'n' tease... or, rather, Unity Diner in London is calling it that and I borrowed it because it is a perfect name (thank you for being so imaginative). The sauce consists of various vegetables, so not only is it great for adult skeptics but it's also great for picky eaters.

Ingredients

- 2 medium/large potatoes
- ½ an onion
- 1 carrot
- 1 cup oat milk
- 1 clove of garlic
- 2 tablespoons nutritional yeast
- 1 tablespoon flour
- ground nutmeg
- 1 teaspoon turmeric
- 1 pinch cayenne pepper
- pasta of your choice

Cut the potatoes, onion, and carrot into smaller pieces and boil them until they are soft enough to eat. Then put them in a blender with the oat milk and blend until the sauce is smooth. Then add garlic, yeast, flour, and the rest of the spices and blend again. If the consistency seems too thin, add a bit more flour, and if the consistency is too thick, add a bit more oat milk. Boil your preferred pasta until it's al dente, place it in an oven-proof tray with the sauce on top, and mix well. Then place the tray in the oven for 5 to 10 minutes at 350 degrees Fahrenheit. It can be served with a side of broccoli, which I personally really like.

Pasta Salad with Curry Dressing

For two people

Ingredients

- 1 cup pasta (I can recommend using the lasagna sheet trick)
- 3 tablespoons vegan mayo
- ½ teaspoon onion powder
- ½ teaspoon garlic powder
- 1 tablespoon freshly chopped parsley
- 1 teaspoon curry powder
- (a pinch of turmeric is optional)
- ¼ cup shredded carrot
- ¼ cup shredded squash
- romaine lettuce
- spinach
- cucumber

Start by boiling the pasta. It will have to cool before it can be added to the salad, so it's a good idea to get that out of the way first. The dressing is based on one of my basic dressing recipes, which I use for basically everything, just with curry added. Mix the vegan mayo with a ½ teaspoon of water or plant milk. You can adjust the consistency so it matches your preferred dressing type; however, make sure to not make it too thin. Then add the onion and garlic powder, as well as the parsley and curry powder. Stir it all together and add salt and pepper to taste. You can also add a dash of turmeric, which does not add a lot of flavor but looks really nice. Now mix your preferred salad. I usually choose carrot, squash, cucumber, and romaine for mine. Add your dressing and the cold pasta on top and mix.

The pasta salad is a great, quick lunch meal on the go and can easily be transported in a jar or a lunchbox. I have often brought it to barbeque nights, along with some vegan sausage. If you store the salad in a jar in the fridge, it can stay fresh for a couple of days.

Beet Wellington

For four to six people

This is the main holiday dish that I have made for the last three years, and it's a favorite in my family. Oddly enough, it does not call for beets in the recipe, which makes the title a bit misleading, but I cannot stay away from an obvious pun. It can be a bit difficult to hold on to your sustainable dietary choices during the holidays; trust me, I know. But you can also trust me when I say that it really, really helps to have some delicious green alternatives right at hand; something crispy, something fatty, something salty, that way you are much more likely to actually stick to your plant-based food. I also want to use the opportunity to mention that the first time I made this for my dad, he said that it tasted better than the holiday roast, and that is a compliment I still cherish. So if you don't believe me when I say that this is just as good as traditional holiday dishes, then trust my sixty-one-year-old dad. If he didn't need a holiday roast, neither will you.

Ingredients

- 10 oz of plant-based minced "beef," homemade or a store-bought soy/pea alternative
- ½ cup chopped mushrooms
- ½ cup finely chopped walnuts
- ½ cup finely chopped almonds
- ½ cup olive oil
- 2 chopped cloves of garlic
- 1–3 bay leaves
- 1 tablespoon ground juniper berries
- 1 tablespoon rosemary
- 1 tablespoon thyme
- salt and pepper
- ½ cup chopped parsley
- ½ cup pickled red cabbage
- 3 sheets of savory puff pastry dough

Fry the mince vegan filling with mushrooms and nuts. Remember to use oil and a bit of water to avoid it being too dry. Then add garlic, spices, parsley, and red cabbage. When everything is mixed nicely, get an oven-proof tray and coat it in a vegan butter or oil. Take the sheets of puff pastry dough and roll them out on a well-floured surface so that they have the right measurements. You want to aim for 6 x 10 inches. Put them next to each other so they make one large sheet and use a bit of water to "weld" them together. Shape the minced filling in the middle of the pastry sheet so it looks like a big sausage—take your time and make sure the filling is even in size and shape on both ends. About 2 inches from the filling, cut the dough into pieces on each side. Now drag the pieces over the filling one at a time in a braid pattern. It looks so pretty, and it also makes the dough rise more. The excess dough can be used to make small decorations on the side of the roast. Check that both ends are sealed shut. When

your roast is done, coat it in vegan cream or oil and place it in the
oven for 20 to 25 minutes at 400 degrees Fahrenheit. Serve with
traditional seasonal side dishes.

Problems with Popular Plants

When discussing healthy and sustainable food, we often end up
generalizing a fair bit. It can be easy to deem all animal products
equally bad and all plant foods equally good, but in reality, it's a lot
more nuanced than that. Now we're going to explore some of the
nuances of plant foods, and hopefully this will be helpful when making
conscious decisions in the future. We have already established that
soy production can be extremely harmful to the planet, primarily
because of the vast quantities we're producing—and that is the
case with other plant foods as well. Increased demand for certain
types of food on the Western market has resulted in consequences
for the local communities and areas that are responsible for the
production of these products. These issues include, but are not
limited to, deforestation, monoculture, forced labor, forced child
labor, and destruction of natural habitats. Does that mean we should

never, ever buy these products
again? Of course, all these
decisions are yours to make,
but it's definitely a good idea
to reduce the consumption
of these goods, at least to
some extent, and in doing
so, make them fit for special
occasions rather than everyday
occurrences. Zero-waste
living is, in a lot of instances,
about refusing to support some

industries completely while reducing the consumption of others. It should also be noted that it is indeed possible to find companies that produce these products significantly better, more sustainably, and more ethically than others, and a good rule of thumb for zero waste is to look to support smaller companies and farms rather than big corporations. Often, this is not only more sustainable, but it can also strengthen smaller communities and provide more transparency in the supply chain.

Avocado: The avocado has grown immensely in popularity over the years, and the growing demand comes with a price. Mexico is the world's biggest supplier of avocados. However, the growing demand has resulted in serious consequences for Mexican farming communities. The production has led to illegal forest fires and a large part of the avocado industry is controlled by cartels (which sounds wild, I know). A more sustainable alternative would be to consume avocados in smaller quantities, support local, independent farms, and replace the avocados with other veggies.

Cocoa: Personally, I have stopped buying chocolate and cocoa products that are not Fairtrade certified, and when I can only afford the cheapest options, I choose to go without. Several studies show that 75 percent of the cocoa industry has a destructive effect on biodiversity in the areas where it is grown. With this also comes the opaque supply chain. A study by Cocoa Initiative in 2018 showed that 2.1 million children were working in the West African cocoa industry. Similar studies confirm the same issue in other industries, like sugar production, as well. Because of this, Fairtrade can be a helpful tool with which to navigate what products to buy and what products to avoid.

Coffee: The cultivation of coffee itself is not as impactful as one might think. The coffee industry uses relatively few pesticides because the coffee plant has its own built-in protection from animals and insects—caffeine, to be precise. The significant impact of coffee comes primarily from the processing of the coffee beans, because it is only 22 percent of the plant that can be used for consumption. Additionally, there are transportation emissions, but another large part of the impact is packaging. A lot of coffee products are shipped and bought in capsules that are served in plastic. There is also the impact of coffee accessories, like plastic sticks for stirring. If you want a more sustainable coffee routine, it is a good idea to choose organic coffee, drink it from a reusable cup, avoid capsules and single-serving products, and reuse coffee grounds as body scrubs. (Psssst, it is also great in a compost.)

Palm oil: At this point, it is not uncommon knowledge that palm oil can be a problematic ingredient, because the problems with palm oil are far from new. This is one of the most frequently used ingredients in processed foods like most snacks, bread, sweets, cakes, and chips. Furthermore, palm oil is also a common ingredient in many cosmetics, as well as in biofuel. The majority (85 percent) of conventionally produced palm oil comes from Indonesia and Malaysia. When growing palm oil, the wet fields must be drained in order to be optimal for the farmers, and when this happens, the previously wet areas, such as bogs, will start to emit previously stored CO_2 into the atmosphere. To put this issue into perspective, the combined CO_2 emissions from the palm oil industry account for 6 percent of all global emissions. The impact of the palm oil industry is also recognized to be the primary reason for the vast deforestation of natural areas in Indonesia, a process which has resulted in the extinction of several species of flora and fauna. The industry presents a large problem because not many companies who utilize the product take responsibility for its production and, thus, see no reason to rethink or phase it out. As a consumer, it can be difficult to avoid it completely because it is in most processed products and can be listed with over twenty different names on an ingredients list.

Chapter 10

ZERO WASTE ON THE GO

It is one thing to create good and green habits at home, at this point I think many people are trying to improve their home routines to produce less waste, and it is also one of the best places to start. We know our daily routines and thus we often find it easier to prepare and adjust some zero-waste habits for what the day brings. But it gets increasingly difficult when we are going on vacation, when we have a long commute to work, when we are on the go, or for some entirely different reason have to act outside our homes and routines. We generate a significant amount of waste when we transport ourselves, and this is not only related to fuel emissions. The solution is, of course, to never leave your house and only stay within the confines of your personal zero-waste space. Thank you for buying my book, hope you liked it!

Oh, so you aren't satisfied with that solution? Yeah...that is fair. Okay, let's look at some other ways we can deal with this.

When it comes to zero waste in particular, we have to talk about
to-go products and convenience offers. There are countless
products made in travel sizes, as well as easily accessible fast food,
which all weigh in on the final impact of our vacations, trips, picnics,
and general commute. Of course, there is room for improvement, and
you can actually get really far just with a little bit of preparation. This
chapter is for those of you who want to generate less waste
on the go.

Make Your Own Zero-Waste Kit

Much like in day-to-day life, not everyone's routines and needs are
the same. Therefore, it can be an advantage to figure out which
needs and wants you have while traveling. Do you drink coffee? Are
you bringing food on the bus or the train? How long is the trip? And
so on and so on. Once you know your needs, you can start putting
together your own zero waste-kit, which can help you on your way.
Here are some suggestions for what you can put in such a kit:

- **Thermos:** If you like hot drinks, it can be a good idea to bring
  your own heat-proof container. This saves you both the paper
  cup and plastic lid while on the go.

- **Water bottle:** If you like something cold to drink, a reusable water bottle is a nice thing to bring. You can fill it with tap water if it is safe to drink, or use it to buy juice or soft drinks.

- **Canvas bags:** If you know you're going to get hungry and want a snack, like cake, bread, a granola bar, or a sandwich, you can bring a canvas bag to keep it in rather than using the disposable packaging those things are usually sold in. I have also often used a canvas bag for smaller snacks, like nuts or pick-and-mix candy. The bag also doubles as a handy napkin after the meal.

- **Lunchbox:** A lunchbox isn't only handy for homemade sandwiches. It can also be used at salad bars (remember to weigh the box first) or for more liquid foods that do not do well in canvas bags.

- **Cutlery:** If you're eating something that requires cutlery, you can usually only get the wooden or plastic kind on the go, which is why it can be a good idea to bring a spoon or a fork from home. I have a combined device, a spork, and it is always with me when traveling.

- **Straws:** Straws do not need to be plastic. You can get them made from bamboo, glass, or steel. It is of course easiest to completely go without, but if you feel you really need a straw, it is good to pack a reusable one.

- **A glass jar:** By now, my mason jars are all pretty well-traveled. I usually bring one of them with me, since they can serve as a drinking cup, a container for salads, or snack-storage. They are nice and versatile, so you don't need to bring many different containers, especially if you have the option to rinse them out while on the go.

Sustainable Vacations

It isn't only when we're at school or at work that we transport ourselves quite a bit. Many families vacation once a year and some do it even more than that. That is why vacations, and the expenses associated with them, must be a part of our efforts to live more sustainably. There is no need to completely abandon wanderlust and joyful vacation moments just because one wants to live more sustainably, but one has to think about *how* to vacation and how to do better. The following sections will be about how you can travel and see the world in a conscientious and green way. It will touch on everything from tourism and sunscreen to air travel and how you can be a green consumer while in a foreign place.

Great vacations without planes

It is no secret that plane travel weighs heavily on the climate, and I think most of us know that we are not exactly paragons of climate protection whenever we board an airplane. According to the Nature Conservancy, the average carbon footprint for a person in the United States is sixteen metric tons per year, one of the highest rates in the world. Globally, the average is closer to four tons—a direct flight from Denmark to New York produces just about three metric tons of CO_2 per passenger, if the plane is fully booked. If you travel by plane just once every year, the CO_2 produced by that single journey will be a very substantial part of your personal CO_2 production. For every passenger, an airplane produces 138 grams of CO_2 per mile traveled, which is considerably higher than the twenty-seven grams for busses and thirty-seven grams for trains, according to figures published by GreenMatch. But why does plane travel pollute so much? About 40 percent of the pollution comes from the burning of fuel, as it takes a massive amount of fuel to get a plane up in the sky. In fact, a commercial airplane uses one gallon of kerosene, a particularly efficient fuel type, per second. These figures make airplane travel one of the world's biggest polluters, along with oil production and agriculture.

In my experience, plane travel seems to be a rather standard form of travel for many consumers. One might think it is not so strange that airplane travel pollutes as much as it does when people around the world are flying all the time. But it is not at all common for everybody in the world to travel by plane. According to Lund University, only about 3 percent of the world's population regularly fly (that is, travel by plane at least once a year). This means that it is a very small part of the world's population who are responsible for one of the most polluting industries, and that is neither sustainable nor particularly fair, since the consequences affect everyone.

Now, before going further, this is absolutely one of those things where not everybody is able to make the same choices. Some people have to fly for work, or to see family members, and obviously I would never advise someone to never see their family again because of the carbon footprint traveling has. It is also worth noting that the options for public transportation are not the same everywhere in the world, which absolutely affects consumers' decisions to fly. This is surely an industry that needs to take more responsibility, and the option for public transportation is also something that should be prioritized much higher by governments. If you can skip the flight and opt for lower-impact traveling, then do that. If you cannot, then fly minimally, use carbon offsetting, do any of those small things to slightly lessen the impact, but also know that the fact that you do not have more sustainable options for transportation is not your fault. I want you to focus on the positive changes that you can make, and not obsess over those things that are out of your control. Use that energy in more constructive ways.

In 2019, I stopped flying. In the past, I have flown quite a bit, both for work and for vacations, and that was not particularly green of me—especially not when there are alternatives. I chose to challenge myself and my convenience because that is, essentially, what airplane travel is. We want to go from A to B very quickly and the journey itself is no longer that important. Instead, it is just something that needs to be over quickly. When you stop flying, all travel takes a fair bit longer, and for many, this isn't a very appealing notion. Last year, I had to travel from Copenhagen to Brussels, a trip which, by plane, would have taken about an hour and a half. But without a plane, you can take the train or the bus to Brussels. To avoid having to spend the night in the middle of Germany, a night bus seemed like a good option. The trip became a thirteen-hour journey on the German, Dutch, and Belgian highways, and what a trip it was—friendly and talkative co-passengers, a restroom that only worked for about half the journey, and a bus driver who sold soft drinks out of his personal minifridge and told jokes over the speakers for the entire duration.

I have since tried other long-distance trips without planes, a lot of them starting from Aalborg where I live, and I have learned a lot by traveling this way. First and foremost, I have learned that while I would not say that "it is about the journey, not the destination" (that is a bit of a cliché), the journey can be just as rewarding as the destination. You experience so much that you would not have otherwise, and you end up getting to know the people you travel with. It can be a bit daunting, and I have had my travel anxiety tested (if I'm met with too many unexpected changes and delays, my breathing tends to quicken quite a bit), but I always get there and home in the end. Going by bus often saves you a lot of money compared to plane travel, and if you are just going to another place within the same continent, I thoroughly recommend using busses and trains. For anyone living in Europe, I recommend Brussels to those who want to see more without flying. From there, in just a couple of hours you can go to Paris, London, or Amsterdam as day trips. That is a lot of different cities and sights to see without ever leaving the ground. However, there are still trips which are about as costly as plane travel, if not more so. Taking the train around Europe can easily end up costing hundreds of euros. This is due to, among other things, a lack of demand for affordable long-distance train options because people tend to choose planes instead.

When you decide to stop flying, there are obviously some destinations which are automatically sorted in the "not going to happen" pile, unless you are prepared for a really long trip. Personally, I started out by saying no to planes when traveling to destinations close by, where going by bus or train made just as much sense. Trips that take less than twenty-four hours are pretty easy to deal with. Something I have later thought a lot about is how we always want to travel far away for new experiences. Both in my teenage years and as a young adult, I often longed to go to Bali, Tokyo, or New York, and while I still very much want to go to these places someday, it has dawned on me that there are many places close by that are just as amazing. There are so many places in the northern parts of Europe, essentially my own backyard, that I have yet to see, and I try to remember to appreciate the things around me, instead of dreaming about some far-off paradise on the other side of the globe. I promise you, your side of the planet has plenty of paradise places as well.

If you are traveling by bus or train, I recommend that you bring:

- **a lunchbox** (read the packed lunch section on pg. 143 to see how to make that zero waste);

- **a water bottle** or another kind of refillable container for liquids;

- **a power bank,** which is really handy, so you don't run out of battery on the autobahn;

- **clothes for more layers** depending on the climate inside the bus, and they can be used as a nice pillow;

- **a book,** so you have something to do that does not require power or Wi-Fi;

- **a sleeping mask/eye mask** if you want more of an uninterrupted sleep on the go;

- **headphones,** because regardless of whether or not you listen to music, they're good for shutting out the sound of the other travelers if you need a little space.

Buying green while on vacation

Okay, you are on vacation. No matter your travel situation, you're there now and there are many things you can do to be greener while there. A lot of them will not change your perception of the trip at all, and some will even make it better. The fact is, your vacation will not be made less fun by being greener.

Tools for greener vacations

- **Sunscreen—**or at least most sunscreen—contains a compound called oxybenzone. This has a disruptive effect on the ocean's ecosystem and has been shown to be an endocrine disruptor in fish. It is also directly related to the destruction of coral reefs. Therefore, if you're going swimming, it is a good idea to find a sunscreen that is reef proof.

- **Happy Cow** is an app that can be used to find vegetarian and vegan restaurants in your local area. It is really nifty and user driven, so you can read recommendations and tips from other

users. If you're going somewhere for the first time, it can be a
real lifesaver.

- **CO_2 compensation** is not necessarily the quick guilt-free
  fix we all want it to be, but if you are flying, it is better than
  nothing. Though the best thing to do is not fly, of course.

- **Support the local community** instead of spending money in
  large, international chains and restaurants while on vacation.
  This can be done by eating at local, independent restaurants
  or buying from local artists and artisans instead of large
  chain stores.

Souvenirs

Gifts and souvenirs could, in theory, just have been a part of the
previous section, but there is so much to say here that I think it is
best to give it its own section. Because the things we bring home
from our vacations actually have a pretty large impact and footprint.
By now, it is becoming apparent that whenever we spend money, we
are also given an amount of influence, and this is still true when we
are on vacation. Most vacation destinations have so many tourist
shops and chain stores, and you would think that when you buy
something there, you are supporting the local community, but this
is often not the case. Most often, you are giving your money to a
big international corporation that has outsourced the production
of souvenirs and knickknacks to large factories. Because of this,
it is a good idea to stay far away from the classic tourist shops and
chain stores. Instead, as mentioned in the previous section, you can
support local artisans, artists, musicians, and craftspeople.

You can also bring home souvenirs that you have not spent money on.
Even if you are a sustainable badass, I am not suggesting thievery,
since it would be a bad vibe, but there are many more things of value
than just the ones you can buy. One of my favorite souvenirs is a little

sign I found on the sidewalk in Beijing (before I stopped flying). That sign and a jar of curry were the only souvenirs I brought home from that trip and, today, I have made a fridge magnet out of the sign and look at it every day. You can also find pretty rocks at the beach, a sapling from a plant (if legal), seeds, or a recipe. There are so many options and they don't need to be mass-produced and wrapped in plastic.

Another solution is to buy something secondhand. This has been my go-to when I visit new places in Europe. I already love visiting antique and secondhand stores, and that is where I find most of my things at home, so why not souvenirs? It is really interesting to see what is donated in other cities, and especially in other countries, so that is a strong recommendation from me. From my visit to Siena in Tuscany, I have a beautiful glass jug for balsamic vinegar that I use daily—I bought it in a tiny secondhand store in a basement that was a thousand years old. From Madrid, I have a painting of a beautiful woman made on the back of an old palette, which I had to buy by speaking French, since I cannot speak Spanish to save my life but the man who sold it to me had actually lived in France, and he gave me a discount. In Budapest, I bought a T-shirt in a vintage store behind a vegan restaurant where I ate lunch. I had spilt sweet-and-sour sauce down my clothes, so the replacement shirt became my souvenir. In Germany, I didn't really buy anything, but I did bring bulk pasta with me on the train home.

My point is, deciding to avoid the conventional knickknack shops when you're souvenir hunting isn't just a chance to be greener while vacationing. It is also an opportunity to create great stories and even more powerful memories when you visit other parts of the world.

中国铁通

光（电）缆

电话: 51388000

everything you
can imagine
is real

DU ER
GULERODEN
I MIN RÅKOST

Chapter 11

Waste Free for Parties and Holidays

Did you know that the average person consumes 80 percent more resources during the December holidays than at any other time of the year? In December, the average consumer discards $180 (€160) worth of food. Many consumers want to improve and do better when it comes to everyday sustainability, and more and more consumers are starting to implement green habits and routines. However, it often seems like we forget all our good and green intentions when we need them the most. We don't want to be that person around the dinner table who always has to ruin the good mood by explaining how our gifts are produced, how much food we waste, or how large our overall CO_2 budget is for the holidays—there is nothing *hygge** about that. But what is then? When we're celebrating something and we want to set a good mood, it's rare that we find ways to do it without stuff like gift wrapping, confetti, fireworks, glitter, meat-heavy dishes, and cheap decorations from the supermarket. We know very well that these things are wasteful but sometimes it feels like special occasions and holidays provide us with carte blanche to just buy them anyway—maybe because that is what we have always done. I don't think that *hygge* needs to come with unnecessary pollution

---

* Translator's note: "Hygge" is a Danish word that doesn't translate perfectly into English. It is a noun describing a feeling of coziness, well-being, and contentment, typically while partaking in an activity and usually in the company of loved ones.

and overconsumption of goods, so I guess I don't always mind being
that person around the dinner table. I think I have the controversial
opinion that we might actually end up enjoying special occasions
more if we start consuming less. Therefore, I have dedicated this
chapter to explaining all the hows and whats of sustainable, yet
festive, celebrations and holidays.

Ways to make your holiday season more sustainable

- Choose plant-based versions of your traditional holiday
  foods, even if it just means swapping out the butter or
  cream for plant-based versions.

- Donate food and blankets to local food shelters
  and charities.

- Find ways of giving more sustainable gifts, like choosing
  secondhand items or supporting local businesses
  or artists.

- Reuse whatever you can: containers, packaging, gift
  wrapping or décor. Reuse year after year.

- Buy seasonal décor in thrift shops if possible, and save it
  to use again the next year rather than buying new.

- Have a conversation with your loved ones about shifting
  the focus of the holidays away from gifts and the
  material outcome to experiences, creating memories,
  and being together.

- Avoid excessively wasteful activities or single-use décor
  like fireworks, glitter, and confetti.

Gifts

We give gifts to show the people in our lives that we care about them, and there is absolutely nothing wrong with that. The problem is not the fact that we give gifts, the problem is the type of gifts we give. We buy electronics, clothes, perfumes, and toys—most of which are very likely produced in the same ways described in the Chapter 7 on fast fashion. When we buy stuff in shops and department stores, we signal to the industries that are responsible for the production of these items that we want more, and by extension, that more stuff needs to be produced. So when we think that stores and brands should stop making new stuff all the time, that they should stop overproducing, it's a really good idea to stop buying from them, because that is exactly why it is happening. Instead, it is a good idea to look around for gifts which both the receiver and the planet can benefit from.

The homemade

I have often made homemade gifts and people have always loved them (or…at least they have always told me that they love them, but that is also something!). You can use some of my recipes for care products and make a lip scrub or a lotion—super good gifts, in my opinion. You can also make a cake mix by mixing the dry ingredients for recipes in a nice jar. This way, the receiver need only add water or plant milk. You can also knit, take photos, give plants, or something else if you have a crafty skill.

The pre-loved

These don't sound as awesome as they are, but pre-loved gifts are where it is at. When I am giving a gift to a person who has a register or a wish list, I will find what they want secondhand (especially if I know this person would not appreciate a homemade lotion or a plant). You can use online secondhand platforms like Facebook Marketplace, Depop, Craigslist, Zadaa, Threadup, and so many others depending on where you live. You can find secondhand platforms where you can search for specific items like brands, styles, and models—this is really handy when finding a gift to suit a specific wish. For smaller presents, I simply hit up thrift shops and flea markets in my local area. This is how I usually find gifts for my family—and where they find gifts for me. For the longest time, I have preferred the secondhand hunt over department stores, and even in high school, my best friend gave me a homemade gift voucher to "go crazy in a thrift shop"—a gift that I highly recommend!

The experience

Give a gift that cannot be wrapped: an experience. It can be anything
from a trip to the movies to a wine tasting, concert tickets, sports
events, or a restaurant visit. There are literally no limits when it
comes to experiencing gifts, and all you need to do is write a card.
Perhaps it's tempting to buy one of those prepackaged experience
box gifts, however, they're usually wrapped in plastic. It is much
better to just make the "gift voucher" yourself.

Gift Wrapping

But it's not only what we give that is an issue, it is also how we wrap
it that contributes to pollution. Americans spend $2.6 billion on
wrapping paper a year, and before we write it off as a minor issue that
the wonderful recycling system will take care of, most gift wrapping
is unrecyclable because it's treated with plastic or glitter coatings.
But, of course, there are other solutions.

Do like Grandma

Save the gift-wrapping paper from gifts that you receive from friends or family. Unwrap your gifts carefully and save the paper for a time when you need to wrap a gift. This is a great solution if you receive a gift, because waste is not waste until you waste it. With that outlook, you'll have zero wasted opportunities (See what I did there?)

Refuse gift wrapping

Tell your friends and family that you don't want your gifts wrapped. And you can use the occasion to use sustainable wrapping on your own gifts; this way, you're not just telling other people what to do, you are also leading by example.

Use what you already have

Whether that is a fabric bag, a kitchen towel, or some old newspaper—the most sustainable option is the one you already have. I often wrap my gifts in fabric materials, and if the recipient does not want to use the fabric afterward, I get it back so I can reuse it for another gift. Using what you have works great for everything: paper, ribbons, décor, and cards. Furthermore, wrapping gifts in reusables will also exclude plastic glitter and shiny unrecyclable coatings.

The big holidays and special occasions that we hold so dear are always influenced by lots of traditions and emotions, and therefore it can be difficult to change everything at once. It can be difficult for yourself, but it can also be tough getting the family on board. I recommend starting with yourself because, like with every kind of change, it comes easiest and more successfully when we start by looking at our own behavior. Shop for décor secondhand or make your own, or alternatively, there is so much festive décor in thrift shops, especially around the holidays, all of which is just waiting to be picked up by someone. Research green recipes and food options and aim to replace meat-heavy dishes with lighter and more sustainable alternatives, or practice wrapping gifts with fabric and string rather than using tape and paper. In my own experience, it always helps when you initiate a wish for change by changing your own behavior. For my first zero-waste Christmas in 2015, I asked to not have my gifts wrapped in paper and I brought my own nut roast to the table. Slowly and gradually my family has adapted to my change, and now we all give sustainably wrapped gifts. My parents shop for secondhand gifts for me and my brother, and my dad especially loves the thrift hunt. They also wrap gifts in reusable containers that we can use around the house. "If *you* don't have a need for more towels, *I* can certainly use them" is now a pretty common phrase in our household.

Chapter 12

PLASTIC-FREE CARE PRODUCTS

Oral Hygiene

Teeth care and general oral hygiene is not something I would ever compromise on; however, most toothbrushes, toothpaste, dental floss, and mouthwash are wrapped in layers and layers of plastic packaging. Luckily, there are alternatives, but they have yet to become widely available in conventional supermarkets—so we have to look elsewhere. Toothbrushes made from bamboo or wood are becoming increasingly popular and will help you reduce your use of plastic, both in terms of the product itself and its packaging. The bristles of most bamboo or wooden toothbrushes are still made of new or recycled nylon, which is a type of plastic. However, they're still less impactful than plastic brushes. Toothpaste is a different story. It can be difficult to shop for the alternatives, but they're out there.

One of the first homemade products I experimented with was homemade toothpaste made from coconut oil and baking soda, but I did not like that one bit. The last couple of years, I have used tooth tabs. These tabs taste and look like mints, but when you chew them, they turn into a paste you can use to brush your teeth. They often come in paper packaging or reusable glass containers and can be found both with and without fluoride. When  it comes to mouthwash, I recommend oil pulling. Here you rinse your mouth with oil and this has many of the same benefits as store-bought mouthwash. The oil I am currently using is from Georganics and comes in glass bottles. Dental floss and sticks are great when taking care of your teeth, and there are several products that replace the conventional plastic ones, two examples of which are plant-based floss made from compostable materials and toothpicks made with bamboo or wood which can also be composted and have a much smaller impact than plastic in the long run. I have not found a fully reusable product here, so they are still single use. However, I often reuse them a couple of times before composting, simply by rinsing them with water in between uses.

Shaving

In reality, we really don't need to shave, no matter who we are, and choosing not to shave is naturally a-okay. It is 100 percent up to you as an individual whether or not you remove your body hair. However, I do think that it's important to mention shaving, because there is a lot of potential waste related to hair removal. Everything from packaging to disposable razors, creams, and other products, because they add up. Luckily, there are completely waste-free ways of removing hair— for instance by using a safety razor. This is a kind of old-timey razor made from stainless steel for which you only replace the metal blade. The reason this is less wasteful than the ones you find in most conventional supermarkets is because a safety razor can last you a lifetime. Most disposable, or at least plastic, razors are often heavily

packaged; however, the blades for the safety razor are often just wrapped in a small piece of cardboard. The safety razor works for every person, no matter sex and gender, and can be used in all areas of the body. Furthermore, while the safety razor costs more than a disposable razor at first, it will quickly become much cheaper since you don't have to replace it constantly. Of course, there is also the matter of shaving soaps and gels. A zero-waste alternative is simply a solid shaving soap or a normal piece of solid hand soap—this works great for face, arms, legs, and anywhere in between.

Soap Guide

At this point, liquid soap seems to be a lot more widely available than solid soaps, and of course, there are some great benefits to liquid soaps since they're easier to use in daily life. However, liquid soaps also come with a large amount of plastic packaging and that is a bit silly. The alternative to this issue is right in front of us: a good ol' solid soap block. There is nothing modern or fancy about this solution, it just works. Replace store-bought liquid soap with a solid soap bar or make your own liquid soap at home with a solid soap bar. This is how we avoid a lot of unnecessary

waste. In zero-wasteland, there are several products and methods you can use which do not involve plastic containers with liquid soap and shampoo. Personally, I have spent the last five years figuring out what is the perfect fit for me and that is a shampoo/conditioner soap bar. The solid piece of soap is made wet in the shower and then applied to your hair. You can find these soap bars in many health stores, eco stores, and online. The most famous soap bars are from the soap giant Lush, however, if you want to avoid perfume, and perhaps support local businesses, you can look up health shops and soap makers in your country or area. Dish soap can be trickier to find but you can also get a zero-waste solid dish soap online as well as using bulk options if you have those.

A solid soap tip

When your soap bar is just about
finished, save those small brittle
pieces of soap that are left in a jar.
When you have enough small pieces
you can melt them together and form
your very own Franken-soap. Trust
me, when it comes to tips about zero-
waste soap, this one is...solid! (See
what I did *there*?)

Periods

People who menstruate use an average of 16,000 single-use period
products in their lifetime. Many of these products end up in landfills
or in the ocean, and they're rather resource intensive to produce.
Both disposable pads and tampons are made, primarily, from cotton
and polyester (a.k.a. plastic) but also contain synthetic perfumes and
bleach. So if you get periods, it's a great idea to look into more
sustainable and reusable options. I have a couple of ideas to deal with
this in a zero-waste manner: The first is a menstrual cup. They have
become increasingly popular, and for a good reason. The cups are
made from silicone and can be reused over and over. Actually, a cup
can be used for six to twelve years depending on how you maintain it
and what brand it is. When using a cup, empty it every four to six
hours, wash it with cold water, and reinsert. In between periods, you
sterilize it by boiling it. You generate significantly less waste during
your period when using a cup than when using single-use products.
But there are other options as well. You can also get, or make,
reusable tampons and pads composed of 100 percent cotton. They
work the exact same way as disposable products but rather than

throwing them in the bin, you wash them. Rinse them in cold water and dry them before washing them with the rest of your laundry. The last option I want to include is period pants or period underwear. This option is the least invasive one and does not require you to insert anything. The underwear consists of an absorbent layer of fabric, between three or four other layers, so they do not leak. Their efficiency can vary, but on average they absorb the same as four to six tampons. Rinse and dry after use, before washing with your other laundry.

DIY Makeup and Beauty Tips

When I started learning about the zero-waste lifestyle, I quickly started making my own makeup. I did that because the things listed on the back of my store-bought makeup, and the packaging it came in, did not make sense to me. I had no clue what I was using on my skin. When I was in my teens, I wore as much black eyeliner as I could get my hands on, and not just on my eyes—my lips, eyebrows, and cheeks got the same treatment. My mom would always tell me that

I could not use something on my skin that I was not comfortable eating, and although skin care and cosmetics are a little more complex than that, I did not understand what she meant until I started to look more critically at what I was consuming. I do not want to use anything on my skin if I don't know what is in it. However, navigating the ingredients list of a beauty product is far from easy breezy. Until this point, I did not realize that all the products I used on my skin and in my hair would eventually end up in our natural environment. But that is exactly what is happening; when we wash off makeup, shampoo, sunscreen, or anything of the like, the synthetic ingredients don't biodegrade in water, instead they bio-accumulate. They can also react with other chemical components and create damaging reactions which cause harm to natural ecosystems. These synthetic components and ingredients in our care products act just like microplastic—they never disappear, and they start piling up. Therefore, I decided to try to make my own products.

Homemade Body Lotion

Ingredients

- ½ cup coconut oil
- ½ cup cocoa butter
- ½ cup shea butter

The first thing I made was my own lotion. It is easy, cheap, and significantly more sustainable than buying fancy, prepackaged lotions from big beauty brands. The lotion stays fresh for months because it's basically just oil. I also really like to give the lotion as gifts, both for friends and family, and everyone has, so far, been super excited about trying it out. I found all my ingredients in Isangs, a soap shop in Copenhagen where they only sell organic and Fairtrade products without plastic packaging. Melt the three oils in a double boiler and stir until they have melted together completely. Remove them from the heat and pour the oil into a bowl. Place the bowl in the fridge and wait until the oils are no longer transparent—it should start to look like a yellow-green solid mass after 20 to 40 minutes. When the time is up, take the bowl out of the fridge and whisk it until the oil stiffens like meringue. It usually takes 2 to 4 minutes. I recommend using an electric whisk if you have one, but it can also be done by hand. The lotion will feel light and airy when it's done, however, if you overwork it, it can start to thicken up a bit. Do note that it still works great as lotion even if it's overworked. Transfer your lotion to a jar with an airtight lid. When you want to use it, scoop out a tiny bit of lotion and warm it slightly with your hands before applying.

Homemade Setting Powder

Ingredients

- arrowroot powder
- cocoa powder

This powder works a bit like a mild setting powder. When I initially made it, I was a bit skeptical, but it proved to do exactly what I hoped it would. Arrowroot powder is a type of starch and can be bought in many health shops, and it's used in many of my makeup recipes. Fun fact: it is also excellent for smoothing out sauces and gravy. Arrowroot contains both vitamin B and potassium. Take a teaspoon of arrowroot powder and add cocoa powder until the desired skin tone appears. After that, it's ready for use. You can of course also mix a larger portion and store it in a jar. In that case, simply stir it quickly before use.

Homemade Concealer

Ingredients

- 1 tablespoon arrowroot powder
- cocoa powder
- 1 tablespoon bentonite clay
- 1–3 teaspoons soy wax
- 1 tablespoon lotion

Firstly, you will have to make a setting powder from arrowroot and cocoa which matches your skin tone. Follow the directions in the previous recipe. When you have your powder, mix it with 1 teaspoon of bentonite clay, which can be found in soap shops and several health shops. Then add melted soy wax and lotion as well. Mix all the components in a small dish or a bowl and stir with a chopstick or a toothpick. When thoroughly combined, transfer into an airtight container and let it rest for 20 to 30 minutes in the fridge before use.

Homemade Blush

Ingredients

- 1 beetroot
- arrowroot powder

This homemade beetroot blush smells heavenly, and it looks amazing and pigmented. I do think that it's important to mention that it works best on top of a layer of foundation, concealer, or powder. Otherwise, it does not have much to hold on to. Making this blush can be an exercise in patience because it involves sun-drying beets. Cut the beet into thin slices, lay them on a piece of paper or fabric, and place it in the sun, near a window for instance. It can take a couple of days for the beets to dry completely. You can also use your oven or a dehydrator for that matter. Set the oven to the lowest possible temperature and dry them for 2 to 3 hours. If you use the oven, make sure to keep an eye on them, though, so they do not burn. I recommend using the sun, as it also saves on electricity. When the beets are completely dry, grind the beets to a fine powder in a mini food processor or a coffee grinder. The powder is super pigmented, so make sure to find a storage container that seals tight. Mix your beet powder with arrowroot until you reach the desired shade of pink.

Homemade Lip Tint

Ingredients

- 1 beetroot
- 1 tablespoon soy wax
- 1 tablespoon coconut oil
- 1 pinch of activated charcoal or cocoa powder

Of course you can make your own lip balm. It is not as difficult as you might think. Firstly, mix your own blush by using the previous guide or by using a blush you already have. Now take a small double boiler and melt your soy wax and coconut oil. Find a good, designated mixing stick and add the blush little by little. Initially, the lip balm will turn very pink when using a blush, but if you want a darker shade, you can add charcoal or cocoa. Experiment with the nuance by adding tiny pinches of color until you find the shade that is perfect for you. Store the lip balm in a flat container and apply with a brush or your finger.

Homemade Eyebrow Tint/Eye Shadow

Ingredients

- 1 tablespoon arrowroot powder
- 1 teaspoon cocoa powder
- 1 pinch of activated charcoal

If you have a natural pigment, you can turn it into eye shadow, which is neat, right? You can find natural dark pigments in cocoa or activated charcoal, which I have both found quite useful when making darker shades, both for eye shadows and eyebrow tints. Start by mixing arrowroot, cocoa, and charcoal until the desired dark shade appears. Then transfer into a storage container. Just like the blush, the eye shadow does last longer if it has something to hold on to, like a concealer or a foundation. I always use a fingertip of my homemade lotion before applying my makeup and that works wonders for me.

Homemade Mascara

Ingredients

- 1 teaspoon activated charcoal
- 2 tablespoon aloe vera gel
- 1 teaspoon soy wax

Mascara is something many people use every single day and therefore it's nice to know that there are more sustainable options than the conventional beauty brands. You can also make one yourself as a fun project. This stays good for one to two months. Use aloe vera gel (grow your own plant for extra points) and mix it with activated charcoal. Melt the soy wax over a double boiler and mix it in with the rest. Let the mascara rest for 10 to 20 minutes and then it is ready for use. Apply the mascara with an old, clean toothbrush or an old, clean mascara brush.

Easy Facemask

Ingredients

- banana peel

Nope, this is not a joke people. If you need a quick and easy face mask, rub the inside of the banana peel on your face. It contains loads of nutrients that your skin will love and will leave your face nice and smooth. Moreover, you can also use the inside of the peels for your plants if they lack some shine. Rub the inside of the banana peel against the leaves of your plant, it leaves them (okay, see what I did *there*?) nice and shiny.

Charcoal Mask

Ingredients

- ½ teaspoon turmeric
- 1 teaspoon activated charcoal
- 3–4 teaspoons rose water or distilled water
- 2 teaspoons baking soda
- 2 teaspoons bentonite clay

Mix all the ingredients in a bowl and stir with a spoon or a chopstick. When thoroughly mixed, cover your face with an even layer of the mask but avoid nostrils, eyes, and mouth. Let it sit for 30 to 45 minutes or until the mask is dried up. Then rinse with cold water. You can also use a sponge or a cloth to massage the skin once the mask has come off.

It can perhaps seem daunting and rather overwhelming to produce all your own makeup and beauty products, however, I personally regard them as fun and useful experiments. Some of them I use every day, like my lotion. Others I have made a couple of times but, once I run out, I move on to something else. The most important thing when it comes to zero-waste makeup is to relieve yourself of the idea that we have to use twelve lotions and three eye shadow palettes to look pretty. You do not have to buy tons of things you will not need or finish. A good and simple makeup routine does not necessarily require a whole bunch of stuff and can easily be sustainable. You can also find products in glass or cardboard packaging, rather than plastic, or buy the refill options rather than buying the full packaging. You can also choose products that you know you will be able to use for several things. I like to use my eye shadows both on my eyelids as well as on my brows. I also like to mix my lipstick to create new shades rather than buying more products than necessary.

Products That You Might Want to Phase Out or Stop Buying Right Away

I have made a list of some of those products that we often tend to use, or misuse, and that we might not actually need as much as we think we do (well, we actually do not need any makeup, but one thing at a time). Check it out and see how many you can phase out right now. However, if you already have these things in your house, it is way better to finish them off instead of throwing them away—there is no need to waste them. If you do not feel like using them again, you can also give them to friends or family. My mom got my entire collection of nail polishes, so she did not have to buy new ones for a long time and my old ones did not go to waste. I know it can sound a little harsh, or perhaps unfair, that I get to decide what you need and what you do not—and maybe this is where the cheeky badass part comes into play, who knows? No, of course I cannot decide what you need and what you do not need, and if some of these things bring you immense joy, then perhaps start your zero-waste journey in a place that does not mean so much to you. It took me a long time to phase out some of these items myself, while others I could stop buying right away. This list is not meant as anything more than a source of inspiration and reflection, an idea of the items I personally have found to be unnecessary and wasteful, from my own point of view. All we're here to do is learn how to reflect and review our own consumerism from within. We have to stop perceiving all products and options as tools that are freely available for us to purchase, and instead view them as resources, and we have to ask ourselves if they're really worth it.

Nail polish is rarely plastic free. Partly because of the packaging but mainly because of the product itself, which, for the most part, consists of a synthetic plastic polymer. The sustainable option for nail polish would therefore be to avoid it completely, but luckily, there are tons of other methods of self-expression.

Other nail products also come with the use of nail polish. There are tons of plastic products to be found from nail reels to displays, stencils, glitter, stones, removers, and brushes. A lot of waste is saved by reducing nail polish consumption.

Fake nails are also hard to come by without plastic, so phasing those out might also be a good idea. They are impossible to recycle when they break and simply end up in landfill. Let your own nails grow longer to achieve a similar look. Pro tip: to grow stronger nails, it helps tremendously to leave nail polish alone as well. Use some oil or lotion on them to keep them fresh and healthy.

Specialized lotions come in every shape, variety, and size we can think of. Ever since I made my homemade lotion, that is the only thing I have used, both on my body and my face. Most normal skin types do not need a special night lotion, a day lotion, one for the eyes, and one only for the body. These products generate so much waste, which is unnecessary when most skin types could just use one. Unless you have a medical condition which requires medicinal lotion, or extra sensitive areas, find a good lotion that works for you or follow the recipe from this chapter.

Cosmetic contact lenses are one of those things that might complete your costume, but they might also be quite wasteful. If you want to find other options when trying to imitate eye colors for your costume, try an eye-shadow look.

Glitter makeup is just plastic. Glitter is made from plastic, and when we use glitter products, for instance in makeup, that plastic will fall off and get everywhere—eventually that plastic will end up in our oceans. You can actually get biodegradable glitter, which is a good start, but, for the most part, the sustainable option is to avoid glitter. It is simply not worth the pollution.

Cotton swabs can be found both with and without plastic, but no matter what, they are still quite impactful to produce because they're a disposable cotton product. If you use cotton swabs to clean your ears, a mimikaki stick is a great alternative (which can be bought in some health shops or online). It is an ear cleaner stick that can be used over and over. If you use cotton swabs to correct your makeup, the end of a piece of fabric might do the trick.

Makeup remover often comes in plastic containers as well, and they are super overpriced. Instead, you can use almond oil or coconut oil along with cold water to remove your makeup. These products have tons of nutrients for your skin, they come in recyclable or reusable glass bottles or jars, and we often have them in our house already. Just make sure to rinse all the oil off once you are done. Watch out for your eyes and make sure nothing gets stuck in there.

Makeup remover wipes are another and arguable more wasteful makeup remover product. These wipes are either made from synthetic fabrics (i.e., plastic) or they are made from cotton; but, no matter what, they can only be used once, which is silly when we have other options.

Perfumed sprays like setting sprays and mists, which smell delightful, for the most part serve no real purpose. Often spray mists contain nothing but water and perfume and they are wastefully packaged. Save that packaging by not buying those.

Makeup palettes are super popular, and they always look so beautiful in the stores. But the truth is that they contain an excessive amount of packaging, and we will never use all those colors, anyway. The production of makeup requires a lot of resources, so it is just a waste to buy palette after palette when we only end up using two to three shades. Instead, buy the refill options that you actually use and put together your own palette consisting of makeup you use more often.

Single-use razors are out—it is all about the safety razors, yo!

Hair dye can be super tempting, but think about the chemicals they contain, the plastic packaging, and if it is really worth it. Think about other ways you can change up your look, perhaps with a new haircut or a new style. Often that can do the trick and scratch the itch for change.

Face masks are not all equally bad, but some of them are pretty horrible. The worst kinds are the ones that come with a mask made from polyester or cotton that you put over your face. It is quite wasteful, especially when you can make healthy and sustainable facemasks at home.

Liquid soap, and especially shower gel, is bad. All these liquid soaps and their packaging can be avoided easily by using a piece of solid soap. You can find shampoo, body, and conditioner bars in many places at this point, and they are a great alternative to expensive and overpackaged soaps and gels in bottles.

Makeup brushes and sponges are produced in all kinds of designs and colors, and most of them are quite unnecessary. If you have a handful of good brushes that you take care of and use for different purposes, then you are good. Makeup sponges are made from synthetic materials, so they will never biodegrade, which makes avoiding them a good idea.

False eyelashes should be reconsidered one last time. They are doomed for landfill if they are not lost before getting there. Rather, go for a makeup look and mascara to enhance your eyes.

Cotton rounds are made from cotton (no kidding), and theoretically they can be composted. However, cotton requires a lot of resources to produce, so it is a shame to only use the material once before discarding it. Instead, you can use reusable cotton rounds that you wash between uses.

Chapter 13

I Am Super Green— Now What?

We have the tendency of thinking linearly. It is something we learn when interacting with most aspects of our society. We learn that we go from A to B; it takes time, but at some point we get there. We go to school, we finish school. Then we start something new. We get a job, and slowly we work our way to a promotion. In computer games, we advance in levels after completing tasks, and the intensity of the game increases for every step we take. All these aspects reinforce a linear way of thinking about progress: it's a fundamental way of thinking about life—we set some goals; we achieve them; bam(!), next level. On a slightly gritty and existential note, we're born and then we die. Because of this way of thinking, it is easy to assume that starting a green lifestyle will lead to fulfilling a level or goal in a similar way. Yeah, you would think that for sure. I have been asked this question more times than I can count: "When did you actually become zero waste, you know, fully zero waste?" And I respond to this question with the same answer: "It'll be any day now." The truth is that there is no finish line in sustainability. There is no end goal, no last level. At first glance this might seem very discouraging, because why would you begin something when you have just been told that you will never finish?

It is not with the purpose of discouraging you that I have dedicated
one of the last chapters of the book to this unattainable goal for
sustainability. I want to include this because I think it's important to
remember that we can always learn more; we can always grow. The
whole idea of being an aware consumer is based on the notion that
we keep looking for more knowledge and that we keep adjusting
to the information we find. Even though we have already changed
our habits once, we can still be open to new ideas and perspectives
that we perhaps did not think about the first time. There is a lot to
process, and it's completely up to you where you want to begin your
journey. It does not matter that you are not #ZeroWasteGoals on
the first day; no one—literally no one—is. The most important thing
is to be curious and willing to learn. Having been on this journey
for half a decade and having learned things about many aspects
of sustainability, I am still learning new things all the time, and it is
fucking fantastic. Sometimes it's a challenging path to walk, but
there is no doubt in my mind that it is worth it.

Chapter 14
Guilt Does Not Plant Trees

It is not a secret that we will not have much luck saving the world by ourselves. As a sustainable badass, it is not unlikely that you will meet attitudes like: "We should not pay so much attention to what other people are doing, so you do you and I will do me," "Well, we cannot save the world anyway," or "It is just one bag, it does not make a difference." This attitude comes in a wide range of sizes and colors, and it's equally cringeworthy every time. If you are met with negativity every time you try to do something differently, it can be hard to find the right encouragement. My own experiences tell me that when we try to live more sustainable lives and practice green actions, no matter if it's bringing a canvas bag to the shop or rethinking means of transportation, avoiding fast fashion or cutting certain foods out of our diets, we put a target on our backs. At least, it can feel like that from time to time. Sometimes, I am able to laugh, and honestly, sometimes I make the jokes before anyone else can, but other times it's less fun—other times, the jokes seem a little less light, a little less loving. "Okay, Ms. Vegan, if you care so much about the environment, you should stare into a wall until you die" is an actual thing that an actual person said to me in an actual workplace, without so much as flinching. This is where the smile fades and where the "joke" does not have the purpose of lightening the mood but rather of putting me "in my place." The same goes for the "But you are not saving the world, anyway," remark. This is rarely meant as a constructive tool of debate, and I regard it more as a shield with which someone protects themselves.

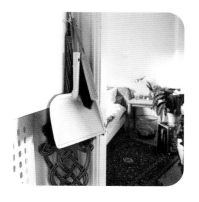 

A lot of people find the motivation to improve their lives and live more sustainably from within—that feeling, almost like a fire, telling us to get our butts off the couch and do something. We can see how the world is changing around us and it gives us a feeling of empowerment that we are able to create change in our lives. It means that a lot of people, myself included, have a lot of feelings at stake when it comes to sustainability. The transition is not mechanical; the complete opposite in fact. It means something to me, just like it means something to loads of other people. It is fortunate and amazing when that fear of losing what we know can be transformed into positive action; however, that is not always the case. Climate anxiety describes a feeling of fear that feels more like complete numbness than like a powerful ability to change. Climate anxiety can creep up on even the best of us, when we want to be as sustainable as possible and create the smallest possible impact. When we are standing in the supermarket and trying to figure out which tomatoes to buy and all the possible aspects of sustainability start to create a brain fog of questions and arguments. There are O2 emissions, transport, greenhouse gases, plastic packaging, pesticides, and water consumption, and sometimes, especially with the influence of anxiety, it feels easier to leave the tomatoes at the store and go home. It can feel completely numbing because we can be so afraid of making the wrong choice that we end up making no choice at all.

It can manifest itself by making it practically impossible to look away from the big picture—from natural disasters, mass migration, global warming, deforestation, and oxygen depletion. When we only look at the big picture, our everyday actions will start to look small and insignificant—then all there is left is to do is nothing at all.

Climate guilt is another concept that I sometimes experience myself and that I see affecting other people around me, as well, especially on social media, where there is a lot of climate shaming happening. Do not get me wrong, I do not think there is anything wrong with criticizing big companies and holding them accountable for their greenwashing. Actually, I think they deserve that treatment. However, when it comes to other people—not big celebrities with tons of influence but just normal people like ourselves, I think the tone can get a little sharp and aggressive. When the way we approach our peers is just as assertive as the way we would have addressed a billion-dollar corporation, I think we have a problem.

If you choose to speak your mind about a certain subject which is relevant in the sustainability discourse, then you often end up with a target on your back and an ocean of whataboutism. Whataboutism is very simply a term that describes when a conversation is derailed by the introduction of a new subject or a completely unrelated question. The effect is often that the conversation shifts its focus or comes to a complete stop. Again, it's an aspect of how we choose to communicate with each other and how we use conversational tools, which can have both positive and negative results. If a spokesperson from a company (or your uncle at a family dinner) tries to criticize a vegan pea-based sausage for its water consumption, it's by all means fair to bring the statistics about animal-based products into the conversation if those are the ones they are defending. Arguments as well as counterarguments can be put into the same box—that box being food products and water consumption, so you are talking about the same issue. However, that is not always how conversations go.

Once I hosted a zero-waste workshop where I was going over the issues of plastic pollution in the oceans and what we as consumers could do to avoid disposable plastic in our everyday lives. I was interrupted by a woman who thought it extremely hypocritical of me to talk about sustainability when I was indeed wearing a cotton dress—because the impact of cotton is in no way small and it requires a lot of resources to produce. Why should she listen to me when I was not perfect? It seemed rather irrelevant to her that my dress was secondhand, because that was not really the point of her question. Her goal was to win.

When you change your habits (and write a book about it), you automatically threaten other peoples' old habits. You signal to them (often without even saying anything, or, like me, saying it kind of loudly) that what they are doing is no longer good enough. That does not feel good (trust me, I know), and it makes people want to clap back. When we feel threatened, we protect ourselves, we become defensive, and it's the most human thing in the world to do. For you and me and everybody who wants to live more sustainably, we have to develop a filter, some thick skin, and an above-average amount of indifference toward jokes and snarky remarks. Of course, sometimes it can also be a good idea to engage in a discussion where we can teach others something as well as learn something ourselves. But we also need the strength to know when a discussion is a waste of time.

With climate guilt, it often happens that the feeling of guilt comes from within. It is often your own voice telling you that what you are doing is not enough. Ignore that voice as well, but just a little bit. Let it know, once in a while, that what you are doing now is all you are capable of. The reason I think we should not completely shut it out is because that voice can also be what drives us forward. However, the external voices of shame, which often come from people who are doing next to nothing themselves? Yeah, do not listen to those at all. We literally do not have time for stuff like that. Shame, guilt, and anxiety sneak up on even the best of us, and it's something that we also must learn to navigate, control, and process. Personally, I live a lot in my emotions, and I still get affected by negativity in certain situations, like when I am dragged into a debate that I do not want to be a part of or when I am used as the butt of a joke. I fight off the guilt and the anxiety in the best way I can, and I tell myself, "Guilt does not plant trees."

Disregarding the fact that sustainability is about more than planting trees, it has become my mantra, and it always pulls me out of an unhealthy mind space. Something I have learned, and which I think it is beyond important to mention in a book about sustainable living, is that it's okay to tell people no. It is okay to announce that you do not want to talk about these issues today. You do not have to engage in every single debate with friends, family, or strangers about climate change. Just because you care, and as a result often end up learning about reports and statistics more than any other person around you, that doesn't mean it isn't still okay to leave conversations you do not want to have. It took me a while to figure that out. I have lost count of how many times I have continued a conversation that just left me tired and empty.

To this, I want to add another thing I have learned, and maybe I was the only person who needed to learn this; perhaps everyone else has it figured out already (if that is the case, that is awesome for you), but if that isn't the case, here is my own hard-won lesson: It is okay to have other interests and hobbies that are not related to sustainability. It is okay to be more than a vegan, more than a zero waster, more than a thrift shopper, and more than an activist. It has been freeing for me to find hobbies without any relation to my interest in zero-waste living. Honestly, I believe that the fact that I have other hobbies keeps me from burning out in my fight for sustainability. In 2019, I started training n martial arts. Did I know anything about the sport prior to starting taekwondo? Heck no. I just needed to be more than my work with zero waste, and I was afraid I would burn out, as many activists often do, and that I would become indifferent to the issues.

This is, in and of itself, another aspect of guilt, I am sure. Burning out and losing the passion that drives you is a risk you are running when you dedicate all your time to just one thing, especially if you do not grant yourself a break here and there. If you experience burn out, then you will not be able to help save the world—you will not even be able to save your own backyard in such a state. We do not all need to fit perfectly into the same box. In sustainability, there is room to be different and to expand your perspectives in a direction that you are passionate about. People are different, and focusing on different things and evolving gradually into different people is okay. It took me a long time to refuse the idea of the "stereotypical environmental activist." Zero waste is not a hat that you need to wear all the time, every second of every day; it does not have to be the first thing people notice about you, and it does not have to fully define you. No, zero-waste living is more like a vest. It is fitted for each individual person to wear, there is room to breathe (it is more like a *zero vest*...sorry, the bad puns will be over soon, I swear), but honestly, remember that while we are being good to our planet, we also have to be good to ourselves. Technically, we also have to be good to other people (no matter how wrong we know they are about climate change). No one ever learned anything from being punched in the face with a book. Granted, no one should get medals just for showing up either, so take a deep breath, give yourself a hug, pull up your sleeves, and let us get to work.

Works Cited and Sources

Arthur, Rachel. "Bitter chocolate: Primates wiped out in many Côte d'Ivoire areas—where illegal cocoa farming is on the rise." *Confectionery News*, Apr. 9, 2015. https://www.confectionerynews.com/Article/2015/04/10/Bitter-chocolate-Primates-wiped-out-in-many-Cote-d-Ivoire-areas-where-illegal-cocoa-farming-is-on-the-rise

Astiera, Marta, Yair Merlín-Uribe, Laura Villamil-Echeverri, Alfredo Garciarreal, Mayra E. Gavito, and Omar R. Masera. "Energy balance and greenhouse gas emissions in organic and conventional avocado orchards in Mexico." *Ecological Indicators* 43 (Aug. 2014): 281–287. https://doi.org/10.1016/j.ecolind.2014.03.002

Bakker, Tyra: "The Environmental impact of Cosmetics Production"

Balch, Oliver. "Child labour: the dark truth behind chocolate production." *Raconteur*, June 20, 2018. https://www.raconteur.net/corporate-social-responsibility/child-labour-cocoa-production/

Bech, Jørn, Techinical Institute, sustainable plastic: Worth to know about bioplastic"

Calderwood, Imogen. "16 Times Countries and Cities Have Banned Single-Use Plastics." *Global Citizen*, Apr. 25, 2018. https://www.globalcitizen.org/en/content/plastic-bans-around-the-world/

Concito, Denmark's Green Think Tank. "Freedom to act sustainably." 2012.

Concito, Denmark's Green Think Tank: "Sustainable food."

Copenhagen Municipality (Københavns Kommunes): "sortering af bioaffald."

The Danish Society for Nature Conservation: "Research: Bottom-dragging gear emits large amounts of CO_2 into the ocean." May 12, 2021. https://www.dn.dk/nyheder/forskning-bundslaebende-redskaber-udleder-store-maengder-co2-i-havet/

The Danish Society for Nature Conservation: "Sådan ligger landet." https://www.dn.dk/om-os/publikationer/sadan-ligger-landet/

Davidsen, Ditte Hedegaard. "How To: How your Christmas gift wrapping can save the environment 77,500 tons of water." *Heartbeats*, Dec. 4, 2018. https://heartbeats.dk/how-to-saadan-kan-din-julegaveindpakning-spare-miljoeet-for-77-500-ton-vand/

DoSomething.org

EcoWatch. "640,000 Metric Tons of Ghost Gear Enters Oceans Each Year." Mar. 8, 2018. https://www.ecowatch.com/ghost-gear-oceans-2544526011.html

Engbo, Lisbeth. "People with microplastics in their stomachs." *Plastic Change*, Oct. 23, 2018. https://plasticchange.dk/videnscenter/mennesker-med-mikroplast-i-maven/

Estrada, Orietta C. "The Problem with Palm Oil and What You Can Do About It." *One Green Planet*, 2014. https://www.onegreenplanet.org/animalsandnature/the-problem-with-palm-oil-and-what-you-can-do-about-it/

European Parliament. "Plastic in the sea: Facts, consequences and new EU rules." Last updated Mar. 29, 2021. https://www.europarl.europa.eu/news/da/headlines/society/20181005STO15110/plastik-i-havet-fakta-konsekvenser-og-nye-eu-regler

Eurostat. "Recycling rate of e-waste." Last updated 2018. https://ec.europa.eu/eurostat/web/products-datasets/-/t2020_rt130

The Fish Forward Project. FishForward.eu

Grusgaard, Rasmus. "What types of plastic are there?" *Plastindustrien*. https://plast.dk/hvilke-typer-plast-findes/

Helmenstine, Anne Marie. "Plastic Definition and Examples in Chemistry." ThoughtCo. Last updated Apr. 10, 2020. https://www.thoughtco.com/plastic-chemical-composition-608930

Holmes, Audrey. "How many times can that be recycled?" *Earth911*, Sept. 9, 2021. https://earth911.com/business-policy/how-many-times-recycled/

Miljø- og Fødevareministeriet, *Genanvend*: "metal."

Müller, Adrian. "Comment on Searchinger et al. (2018)'Assessing the efficiency of changes in land use for mitigating climate change.'" *FiBL*, Dec. 18, 2018. https://orgprints.org/id/eprint/34496/1/mueller-2018-Comment_Searchinger-etal-2018-Nature564-249_18_12_2018.pdf

Pesticide Action Network UK. "Pesticide Concerns in Cotton." 2017. https://www.pan-uk.org/cotton/

Plastic Change. "Beat the Microbead: How to avoid microplastics in care products." Mar. 11, 2019. https://plasticchange.dk/videnscenter/mikroplastik-i-plejeprodukter/

Plastic Change. "Plastic and Climate." May 8, 2019. https://plasticchange.dk/videnscenter/plastik-og-klima/

Plastindustrien: "Bioplastic." https://plast.dk/tema/bioplast/

Rauturier, Solene. "What are the most sustainable fabrics?" *Good on You*, May 31, 2019. https://goodonyou.eco/most-sustainable-fabrics/

Ross, Andrew. "A perfect storm: the environmental impact of data centers." *InformationAge*, Sept. 17, 2018. https://www.information-age.com/a-perfect-storm-the-environmental-impact-of-data-centres-123474834/

Schwartz, Larry. "7 Types of Plastic Wreaking Havoc on Our Health." *EcoWatch*, Mar. 23, 2016. https://www.ecowatch.com/7-types-of-plastic-wreaking-havoc-on-our-health-1882198584.html

Segovia-Siapco, Gina, and Joan Sabaté. "Health and sustainability outcomes of vegetarian dietary patterns: a revisit of the EPIC-Oxford and the Adventist Health Study-2 cohorts." *European Journal of Clinical Nutrition* 72 (July 2019): 60–70. https://doi.org/10.1038/s41430-018-0310-z

Sims, Linda. *Water Is a Right*, 2020: "The Fast Fashion Environmental Impact: All You Need to Know."

Slavin, Joanne, and H. Green. "Dietary fiber and satiety." *Nutrition Bulletin* 32, no. s1 (Mar. 2007): 32–42. https://doi.org/10.1111/j.1467-3010.2007.00603.x

Søndergaard, Niels. "Bisphenol A: Therefore, the drug is unwanted chemistry in your everyday life." *Forbrugerrådet Tænk Kemi*, Mar. 22 2018. https://kemi.taenk.dk/bliv-klogere/bisphenol-derfor-er-stoffet-uoensket-kemi-i-din-hverdag

State of Green. "New political agreement to ensure a green Danish waste sector by 2030." 2020.

Synnøve Herschend, Sofie, and Mikkel Secher. "Tons of plastic waste disappear: - People imagine that it is recycled." *TV2Lorry*,

Apr. 23, 2019. https://nyheder.tv2.dk/samfund/2019-08-23-tonsvis-af-plastikaffald-forsvinder-man-bilder-folk-ind-at-det-bliver-genanvendt

Times of India. "How much time need to check tanneries' waste." July 11, 2009. https://timesofindia.indiatimes.com/city/kanpur/how-much-time-needed-to-check-tanneries-waste-hc-to-govt/articleshow/4767069.cms

Vesanto, Melina, Winston Craig, and Susan Levin. "Position of the Academy of Nutrition and Dietetics: Vegetarian Diets." *Journal of the Academy of Nutrition and Dietetics* 116, no. 12 (Dec. 2016): 1970–1980. https://doi.org/10.1016/j.jand.2016.09.025

Videnscenter for Allergi. "Chrome and Cobalt." https://www.videncenterforallergi.dk/forskning/aktuel-forskning/krom-og-kobolt/

Winkler, Nana. "Plastic." *Dansk Affaldsforening.* https://danskaffaldsforening.dk/plastik

World Wildlife Fund. "Cotton." https://www.worldwildlife.org/industries/cotton

Yang, Chun Z., Stuart I. Yaniger, V. Craig Jorden, Daniel J. Klein, and George D. Bittner. "Most Plastic Products Release Estrogenic Chemicals: A Potential Health Problem That Can Be Solved." *Environmental Health Perspectives* 119, no. 7 (July 2011): 989–996. https://doi.org/10.1289/ehp.1003220

Yildiz, Ashley Schaeffer. "Palm Oil's Dirty Secret: The Many Ingredient Names for Palm Oil." *The Understory: The Blog of The Rainforest Action Network*, Sept. 22, 2011. https://www.ran.org/the-understory/palm_oil_s_dirty_secret_the_many_ingredient_names_for_palm_oil/

Special Thanks

Jens Damborg Jensen
Emilie Lind Damkjær for her drawings
Christian & Louise Bredvig Fjordside
Stig Ladefoged
Christoffer from Krabbe Photography

About the Author

In 2015, the Danish Gittemarie Johansen switched fashion week,
impulse shopping, big steaks, and frequent flyer's points for a
sustainable and plastic-free life. Since then, she has been making
a living by giving lectures and workshops about sustainable living
for people of all ages, both in Denmark and abroad. With the zero-
waste principles as a foundation, she moves in and out of various
aspects of consumer culture and, with a background in cultural
studies and communication, she utilizes her social media platforms
to broadcast her anti-consumerist message. Gittemarie's passion
for sustainability originates from her own experiences as an average
and curious consumer, which started her journey toward a more
eco-friendly lifestyle. Gittemarie has a master's degree in English and
Cultural Understanding.

Blog: Gittemary.com
YouTube: YouTube.com/gittemary
Instagram: @Gittemary

Mango Publishing, established in 2014, publishes an eclectic list of books by diverse authors—both new and established voices—on topics ranging from business, personal growth, women's empowerment, LGBTQ studies, health, and spirituality to history, popular culture, time management, decluttering, lifestyle, mental wellness, aging, and sustainable living. We were recently named 2019 *and* 2020's #1 fastest-growing independent publisher by *Publishers Weekly*. Our success is driven by our main goal, which is to publish high-quality books that will entertain readers as well as make a positive difference in their lives.

Our readers are our most important resource; we value your input, suggestions, and ideas. We'd love to hear from you—after all, we are publishing books for you!

Please stay in touch with us and follow us at:
Facebook: Mango Publishing
Twitter: @MangoPublishing
Instagram: @MangoPublishing
LinkedIn: Mango Publishing
Pinterest: Mango Publishing
Newsletter: mangopublishinggroup.com/newsletter

Join us on Mango's journey to reinvent publishing, one book at a time.